THE
BARN
DANCE

Also by James F. Twyman

Books

The Art of Spiritual Peacemaking: *Secret Teachings from
Jeshua ben Joseph*
Emissary of Light
Emissary of Love: *The Psychic Children Speak to the World*
The Kabbalah Code: *A True Adventure**
Messages from Thomas: *Raising Psychic Children*
The Moses Code: *The Most Powerful Manifestation Tool in the History
of the World**
The Prayer of St. Francis
Praying Peace: *In Conversation with Gregg Braden and Doreen Virtue*
The Proof *(with Anakha Coman): A Course in Oneness
(also available as an Internet course)**
The Proposing Tree: *A Love Story*
The Secret of the Beloved Disciple
Ten Spiritual Lessons I Learned at the Mall

Films

Indigo: *A Film of Faith, Family, and an Extraordinary Child*
The Indigo Evolution
Into Me See
The Moses Code: *The Movie**

Music

12 Prayers
Ecclesia: *Volume One*
Emissary of Light: *Songs from the Peace Concerts*
For the Beloved: *An Intimate Evening with James Twyman*
God Has No Religion
May Peace Prevail on Earth
The Moses Code Frequency Meditation*
The Order of the Beloved Disciple

***

*Available from Hay House

Please visit Hay House USA: **www.hayhouse.com**®; Hay House Australia:
www.hayhouse.com.au; Hay House UK: **www.hayhouse.co.uk**; Hay House
South Africa: **www.hayhouse.co.za**; Hay House India: **www.hayhouse.co.in**

THE
BARN
DANCE

Somewhere between Heaven and Earth,
there is a place where the magic never ends

JAMES F. TWYMAN

HAY HOUSE, INC.
Carlsbad, California • New York City
London • Sydney • Johannesburg
Vancouver • Hong Kong • New Delhi

Library of Congress Control Number: 2010920159

ISBN: 978-1-4019-2837-7

13 12 11 10   5 4 3 2
1st edition, September 2010
2nd edition, September 2010

Printed in the United States of America

*This book is dedicated to everyone
who loved and cherished Linda:
Ida, Neil, Colleen, and especially Angela.*

INTRODUCTION

Is there really any such thing as a *true story?* If you speak to most detectives they'll tell you that eyewitness evidence is often the most unreliable. If ten different people reported on a crime or an accident, chances are ten slightly different accounts would emerge. We don't always see what's really there, and conversely, we often miss what is right in front of us. The great philosophers have been asking the question since the beginning of time: "What is truth?" It seems it's not as cut and dry as we want it to be.

This book is being published as a novel, though for me it is absolute truth. The events and conversations that are physically provable have been described as accurately as I am capable of describing them. In other words, they really did happen and are easily verified. As the adventure developed, however, the line between what I experienced and what I could actually prove was harder to discern. That doesn't necessarily mean that they were mere fantasies or dreams, or that they didn't have some basis in real fact. Sometimes the things we experience in dreams have more lasting effect than what happens after we sit up in our beds, stretch, and begin the day. Mystics from nearly every tradition have also claimed that what we call the *real world* is really nothing more than a "waking dream," and that there is another world beyond this one that is even more real. I think I visited that *other world,* and that's the story I'm about to describe. It's up to you to decide what you want to believe, but as for me, I believe it all. In fact, this is as close to the real truth as I've ever come.

~James F. Twyman

CHAPTER ONE

Nothing looked familiar as I arrived in downtown Lakeview in August of 2009. Three and a half years had passed since I had first driven through the tiny Oregon town with my daughter, Angela, and her best friend, Heather, who was asleep in the backseat. And at the time, we felt lucky to be alive. Lakeview had been blanketed by thick December snow, and we arrived white knuckled and exhausted after nearly sliding off a 300-foot cliff on State Highway 140. The fact that I was returning under such extraordinary circumstances years later created a dreamlike sensation that crept up my spine like a slow-moving insect I could neither reach nor expel. My arms just weren't long enough, and my muscles were too stiff to make the effort.

Now, except for my suitcase and guitar, the backseat of the car was empty, but I still found myself looking to see if the girls were there, as if no time had passed since that fateful night. It was near the end of a 2,000-mile drive to Oregon following the death of my wife in Chicago, and we did whatever we could to keep the atmosphere comfortable and relaxed. I packed Linda's ashes in the trunk along with the luggage and assorted items Angela didn't want to leave behind. She would probably never return to Chicago again. There was no one waiting for her now, and the reality of her mother's murder was sinking in.

A giant plywood cowboy proclaimed Lakeview the "Tallest Town in Oregon," a credit due to its altitude rather than the size of its buildings. If it had not been for the strange supernatural pull the area had over me I would have never even considered returning. It was as if I'd left a piece of myself behind on that terrible night, and I sensed I would never fully recover from Linda's death if I didn't return and reclaim it. I was haunted by a memory I couldn't shake, and I had no choice but to drive hundreds of miles out of my way in an attempt to exorcise the demons of the past. It was a journey I didn't really want to make, but in the end I knew that I didn't really have a choice.

Searching for a lost slice of my soul wasn't something I had ever done before, and I wasn't sure how to begin. The only thing I knew for certain was where to find the missing artifact—the cliff. It was waiting for me and I knew it, as if I was the subject of its imagination as much as it was mine. I tried to put it all behind me, but there was something missing that I needed to recover. Only the cliff knew where it was, and I was determined to wrestle the information from its tight fist one way or another.

I left Portland the day before and drove as far as Ashland before continuing the journey to Lakeview the following afternoon. By the time I arrived, it was nearly dark, and I knew it made no sense to drive to the cliff before morning. An image of the spot where I almost lost control of the car was burned into my brain, but without sunlight I would never be able to find it again. I was nearly at the outskirts of the town when I saw the Budget Inn, the same hotel we'd stayed at three and a half years earlier, and I pulled into the parking lot without even thinking. It didn't even surprise me when the sensation returned, the familiar feeling of relief from having safely made it through the storm combined with the awareness that the adventure wasn't over. I opened the car door and took a deep breath of the hot mountain air before walking toward the hotel office. There wasn't any reason to put it off, I thought to myself. It was time to finish the bizarre story and finally move on.

The front door made a distinct sound as I entered, enough to alert the man sitting in the office that he had a customer. I could see the back of his solid body and long dark hair from where I stood, and as he turned around, I wasn't surprised to see that he was Native American. He walked up to the front desk without looking at me, pushing the registration form forward with his stout and muscular fingers.

"You looking for a room?" he asked in a broad, unwavering cadence.

"Yes, just for tonight," I answered. "It's just me, so one bed will do."

"You can have a queen bed for $69. A bit less if you have AAA. You a member?"

It was only then that he glanced up at me, and I felt my blood run cold. There wasn't any logical reason for this reaction, only that his eyes possessed an intensity I didn't expect and a tangible force that seemed to grab hold of me. "Yeah, I am," I finally muttered under my breath. "How much does that make it?"

"Brings it down to $59. That okay?"

"Yes, it's fine. I stayed here once before, about three

years ago, and it seemed comfortable enough."

I realized that I was talking more to myself than to him. The energy I sensed when he looked at me was like a lead weight, and I thought that if I kept talking he wouldn't notice how uncomfortable I felt. He finally looked away and the sensation vanished as if it had never been there at all. I picked up the pen and began filling in the information, hoping he didn't realize what was happening to me. He'd already turned around and was filing some papers into a cabinet. It was only then that I realized how truly massive he was. His shoulders were like steel bars suspended between two buildings, and his back was a powerful combination of sinew and muscle. When he turned toward me again, I felt my eyes dart back to the registration form so he wouldn't think I was staring. I didn't know why, but I sensed that it wouldn't be a good thing.

"You're in twenty-three," he said, laying the key in front of me. "We put breakfast out in the morning, if you want to call it that. If that doesn't work, there are plenty of places around where you can get something that's actually cooked."

"I'm sure I'll find something," I said. "Any place you could recommend?"

He looked at me for several seconds before answering, and I felt the discomfort return. "No," he said, then turned around and walked back to the office. I nervously grabbed my bag and walked toward the door, happy to be leaving.

"Where you headed to?" he asked, pulling me back into the room with his question. I turned around and was stunned by what I saw. He looked like a different man, relaxed and smiling rather than the scowl he'd presented seconds earlier. Though his eyes were focused straight at me, I didn't feel the same discomfort I had before.

"I'm heading over to Highway 140," I said as I walked back to the counter.

"What do you mean you're going to the highway?" he asked, maintaining his newfound demeanor. "You're not just going to the highway . . . there must be somewhere else."

"Actually, I really am just going to the highway. About three and a half years ago I drove through there during a terrible snowstorm. I guess you could say that the place left an impression on me. It sounds kind of strange, but I've been feeling this overwhelming desire to go back, and I'm not sure why. I'm going to go there tomorrow, see what I have to see, then leave."

"My name's Victor," he said as he held out his mammoth hand. "I take it you've never been through this area before?"

I reached forward and took his hand, then relaxed and said, "No, that was the first time, and I doubt I'll ever come back. When I came through before, I hadn't realized how dangerous it was. Most of that road seems like it was cut from the side of a cliff."

"It was . . . and it's not a road to mess with. Locals around here call it Suicide Alley because lots of people have gone over the side. But my people had a different idea. For a real long time the ancestors said that the veil between the worlds was thin down there, and that there were a lot of spirits wandering around. In the old days only the holy men or the chief were allowed to go into certain valleys or forests. They would go there to talk to the dead and bring back wisdom. Nobody listens to that anymore, but you can still hear the old people talk about it."

I was stunned by what he was saying to me, as if a piece of the puzzle was falling into place. For weeks the idea of being there again filled my mind, and I thought that if I didn't follow the feeling I would go crazy. Though it made no sense, it felt like a part of myself had been left behind, and I had to find it again and bring it home.

"What do you suggest I do?" I asked, suddenly unsure of myself.

"My first suggestion is to stay away from there and leave," he said, the intense look returning to his face. "Go back to wherever you came from." Then he paused, looking deep into my eyes before continuing. "If not, then do what you have to do then go home as soon as it's done. I'm not trying to scare you or anything, but there are reasons my people believe what they do. I don't know how much of it's true, but these are stories they've been telling for longer than any of us can imagine. I'm talking thousands of years. Beyond that I can't say anything. You go do your thing then forget about it all."

I left the office wondering if I'd made the right decision in coming at all. I was just getting over the terrible grief that had filled my life for over three years, and now here I was chasing something I didn't understand. Part of me wanted to go to sleep then get back in the car and drive to Portland. I knew I wouldn't do that, though. Whatever the feeling was that drew me there, it wasn't going to surrender that easily. One way or another I had to complete this journey and put the whole thing to rest. Only then would I know. Only then would I finally understand.

An hour later I lay in my bed unable to fall asleep. Every time I started to drift off, I saw Linda's face before me, sometimes young and vibrant like she was when we first met in 1984, and at other times dead on the floor of her apartment in Evanston near Chicago. I tried to push the thoughts away, but they didn't want to leave. The last thing I needed was to dwell on that terrible night, the one when everything changed for everyone who loved her. The ceiling of my room seemed to have been painted with sparkles that reflected the light like tiny diamonds, and I tried to focus on them to keep myself awake a little longer. I didn't want to think about her, at least not then, because there was no way I could control the direction my mind might move. *Just don't think about that night,* I thought to myself. *Of all nights, not that one.*

CHAPTER TWO

November 27, 2005
Three and a half years earlier

The air was cool and the single lightbulb hanging above the door cast long shadows down the cement walkway. It was 9 PM and Linda stood next to the low wooden fence that separated her two-story apartment building in Evanston, Illinois, from the house next door. She would regret the moment, smoking a cigarette all the while wishing she were stronger. It had been twenty days, four hours, and nineteen minutes since her last smoke, longer than she had gone in over twenty-five years. From the very beginning her asthma had suffered under the strain, a weakness she had passed on to Angela, her nineteen-year-old daughter. She had meant this to be the time it all stopped, once and for all, and Linda cursed her fragility.

She glanced through the window of the two-bedroom apartment and saw the empty couch and chair, wishing Angela wasn't with her father in Minneapolis celebrating Thanksgiving with his family. She was stupid for saying yes, Linda thought to herself. They always had an agreement, and he had tricked her into breaking it. They hadn't lived together since Angela was four, and had always observed what they called the "holiday rotation law." If he had her for Thanksgiving then Linda would have her for Christmas, or the other way around. The law had worked for fifteen years, but now everything was different.

She had only herself to blame, thinking that it would be nice to spend the holiday alone or with a few friends. She also had to admit that she missed him, too, if only a little. Though they had always been close over the years, she had begun to feel her heart opening again when she saw him, and he didn't waste any time taking advantage of it. Maybe it was unkind to think like that since he had been trying to win her back from the beginning of their separation. She was the one who had locked the door and never even considered a reunion, but he remained steadfast. Linda found the whole thing disarming, and the iceberg was finally beginning to melt. He'd had a couple of relationships over the years, but nothing that lasted more than a year. There was a part of him that wouldn't give up, as if he really meant it when he said that he would always love her. Now, for the first time in many years, she thought that maybe she loved him as well. The wheel of time had begun to work its magic, and Linda found herself thinking that everything might actually work out.

Angela had moved to Oregon to live with her father when she graduated from high school two years earlier. The change had done her some good, and by the time she returned to study at the Aveda Institute in Chicago, Angela was a different person. Her rebellious years of torture and mother-persecution were now behind her, and she seemed more interested in being kind to Linda, even going out to dinner with her mother once or twice a week. She had grown up a little in Oregon, and it was time for them to be friends again. Linda welcomed that news, as if a new age had dawned that she would treasure, one she always wanted but which she had given up hope of ever seeing.

So, why had Linda told Angela's father he could take her to Minneapolis when she knew her daughter would be moving back to Oregon a week later? School was over and Angela decided she liked the small town of Ashland more than Chicago. Her father picked her up after spending a couple of days in the city, and they flew to Minneapolis even though she knew Angela would then spend Christmas in Oregon. That was two holidays in a row. Unfair.

Standing outside, smoking her first cigarette in twenty days, Linda wished she had said no. Why didn't she insist that they both stay, giving herself the chance to enjoy her daughter and their new relationship, as well as the man she had given up hope on so many years before? What better holiday could there have been for such a celebration—Thanksgiving, a time to be grateful for the gifts that surprise a person who long ago stopped looking for surprises? She suddenly realized that that's what she had done without even realizing it—allowed an ancient wound to finally heal and be transformed into something new and useful. Even through the pain of wishing they were there, Linda felt a sweetness she didn't expect. It might not have replaced her need to touch and feel them, but it was precious nonetheless.

They had been twenty-three when they'd gotten married, a decision rushed by the impending birth of their first and only child. No one was surprised when it ground to a percussive stop a few years later, primarily a result of his tortured need to make an impact on the world. He'd left to pursue a career as a musician, and she was left to confront her own abandonment issues, a legacy left by others she had loved. It was like finding the one spot on a person's body that hurts more than any other, then pressing it with vigor. Though he realized his misstep three months later, there was no turning back for her. He had committed the one sin that could never be forgiven, and she wanted him to pay for it. He had gone on to become a well-known, successful musician and author, and had even dedicated much of his career to her, but it didn't matter. The terrible deed had been done, and the impact could not be reversed. Regardless of his penance, the opening to her heart had been closed, and she didn't think she could ever reverse its direction.

Then, to her great surprise, everything changed. Was it simply that they had reached middle age and the promises of youth had been finally laid to rest? A love born in an immature garden had suddenly blossomed to reveal a harvest that was impossible in those early years, and Linda realized that she wanted it more than anything she had ever known. The reward she withheld was now resting in her open hands, and she hoped they would not recoil in fear. Fear, of course, was her constant companion. The man she had known for over twenty years was standing in front of her like someone she had never met before, and it pressed her sense of fairness like nothing else. He had done something terribly wrong, and yet his devotion overwhelmed her righteousness. Could she simply accept laying down her sword and let him pass back into her life without recompense? Or had he already paid his debt, proving beyond reason that his love for her was capable of bearing the test of turmoil and despair?

The cigarette was two-thirds spent as these thoughts ran through her mind, and Linda was getting ready to snuff it in the empty can next to the door. It had been weeks since she'd had to look at that can, and it only reinforced her displeasure. Why did she surrender so easily to the pressures of her life, especially while standing at the threshold of such a promising new existence? Her daughter loved her again, and the man she'd given her life to twenty years earlier was suddenly visible on the horizon. Her aloneness had little impact on these facts, and so it seemed strange that she would resort to these old habits, especially ones that left her feeling so empty. It was time to welcome life in a manner that befitted her new station. It didn't even matter how things turned out in the end, only that she was willing to welcome the approach of a profound shift, one that had the power to transform her entire life.

As she turned toward her apartment, Linda thought she noticed an unusual movement in the corner of her eye, though she couldn't be sure it was anything at all. She didn't think about it again until seconds later she heard the noise. It was a muffled sound, like two men speaking in low tones, not wanting to be discovered. Just to be safe, she quickly reached for the door handle and prepared to return to the safety of a locked apartment.

Her face smashed against the rough wooden surface as they rushed toward her and pushed her hard against the wall. She slid into the window and realized that two men were beginning to push her back into the apartment. Though she still couldn't see their faces hidden beneath dark hoodies, she could tell they were young and dangerous.

The larger of the two had his body pressed against hers, and there was nothing she could do, so she backed into the kitchen with their weight upon her.

A rough hand was pressed against her mouth so she couldn't scream. The men, or perhaps boys, were quick and agile, not wanting to linger too long near windows or the door in case a neighbor looked outside or heard the scuffle. Seconds later they were in the living room with the empty couch and chair, and one man held her while the other shut the shade. Linda tried to twist free, but his arms were wrapped too tightly around her neck and upper body. But then he shifted his weight as he pointed toward the other door, telling his accomplice to make sure it was locked. It was the only opening she would get, and Linda twisted her body enough to free herself from his grip.

Once free, she began screaming as loud as she could. She ran to the window hoping her lungs would shatter the glass. Then she grabbed a book, a large hardcover book she had been reading just before she went outside for her last cigarette. It wasn't a weapon but it was all she had, and she swung it and screamed and hoped someone would come.

Then she saw the knife the other man held. He ran toward her and slashed at her body. Linda's arm deflected the slicing blow but not before being wounded. She kept screaming and hoped someone would hear. The knife came around again, this time cutting into her chest, not deep but enough to make her gasp for breath. Then the terrible man swung his arm and the knife toward her head, and Linda felt its cold steel blade cut deep into her neck. She collapsed to her knees and felt the warm blood flowing down her body. The man stopped, and they both stood looking down on her, wondering what to do next. Linda tried to stand and walk away from them, but the most she could do was crawl. She crawled toward Angela's room, a mother's instinct to protect a daughter who was 400 miles away in Minneapolis. The men fled, not wanting to be there for the end. The wound was too deep, and the blood was flowing too fast. They ran out the door and escaped to the alley, and Linda fell onto Angela's bed.

Chapter Three

I was asleep in my brother's house near Minneapolis when I was startled awake by the sight of my parents standing over my bed. They had that look in their eyes, the one that instantly tells you something's terribly wrong. My mind immediately jumped to Angela. She was asleep in the basement so there was nothing to worry about there. Then I thought about my other brothers and sisters, and nieces and nephews. Had something happened overnight while I was asleep, and now the terrible news was about to surface? The fact that they had traveled the four or five miles to Kenny's house meant that they were rational enough to drive. That meant that everyone in the immediate family was fine. Then my mind expanded the possible parameters like an Internet search engine scanning the computers of the world for the right answer. If not brothers or sisters, nieces or nephews, then who could it be? There was no doubt in my mind that the look in their eyes spoke of something I didn't want to hear—of car crashes and heart attacks, not birthdays and anniversaries.

Looking back, it's amazing to me that I was so rational so quickly after waking up. It was as if my brain switched into hyperactive mode, able to complete complicated mathematical tasks in an instant even though I'd nearly flunked geometry in high school. If it had been a car crash with a child trapped beneath the wrecked auto, I would have been able to lift it clean above my head. It was the physical counter to a purely mental acuity, but the comparison felt real nonetheless. Something terrible had happened and I somehow believed that if I figured it out before they told me then it would soften the blow, perhaps even eliminate it altogether. If I could wrap my mind around it as a concept first, then the reality would be lightened somewhat, making it easier to avoid the crushing blow that was heading toward me.

"What's going on?" I asked as I sat up in bed. "Why are you here so early?"

"Get up and come downstairs," my mother said in a monotone. "We'll tell you there."

That was when the avalanche of fear crushed me beneath tons of earth and gravel. There was always the possibility that I was wrong, that they had just come for an early breakfast and didn't want to wait for me to wake up on my own. Every grain of hope had vanished with the words, "Get up and come downstairs. We'll tell you there." They were like the words of a judge pronouncing a sentence, condemning a murderer to death row, and they struck as hard as Muhammad Ali knocking a shocked and startled George Foreman to the mat.

"Tell me now," I said with a hoarse voice. "What happened?"

There was a long pause before they spoke again, and it drained me of all my strength. I could feel my body going limp, and all the energy I felt seconds earlier escaped through my open mouth. The thought crossed my mind that none of this was happening at all, that I was still sound asleep and dreaming. I had experienced this before, the disconnected and terrible dreams that drift into one's consciousness after sleeping an hour or two too long, the brain's way of saying, "Come on, man, let's get the day going." I remember actually shaking my head to wake up, hoping that I would slowly drift up into a world where my parents weren't looming over my bed with sad and broken eyes, but nothing changed. They were still there, and within seconds I realized the terrible truth—I wasn't dreaming and something really had happened, something so hard and difficult that they couldn't just call. They had to deliver this news in person, whatever it was, making sure they were there for the collapse that would surely follow.

"Mom, what happened?" I asked. "I don't want to go downstairs, so just tell me now."

She took a deep breath. "Linda was killed last night." That was it. It was as if they wanted it to sink in before saying more, giving me the opportunity to adjust to the news that my ex-wife was gone. Of course I knew that it was impossible. I had spoken to her a few hours earlier before going to sleep, so anyone who thought she was killed was ridiculously mistaken. Angela and I had spent the previous day at my sister's apartment, and I'd overheard a conversation she was having with her two cousins, Alissa and Kaitlyn. They were both in their mid-teens, and the way they spoke to their mother reminded me of how Angela had treated Linda when she was the same age. They didn't know I was standing right outside the door and could hear their conversation. It wasn't that

I was trying to listen, but the words I heard come out of Angela's mouth stirred my heart.

"You know, I used to always talk to my mom like you talk to yours," she said, "and my dad always told me I would regret it. I was just like you, all cocky and sure of myself, and I told him that I wouldn't. Well, now I'm a little older and I realize he was right—I do regret it. I wish I hadn't been so mean. So now I'm telling you the same thing. You're going to regret the way you talk to your mom. You probably don't believe me just like I didn't believe my dad, but it's true, and you'll see. I suggest you at least think about it and try to be a bit nicer."

Later that night, when I was back at Kenny's house, I called Linda and told her what I'd heard Angela say. It was like she had been waiting her whole life to hear this news, as if she had given up all hope that Angela would one day treat her with the same love she felt for her daughter. She started to cry, and I knew I had done a good thing telling her. I also sensed that it brought us a step closer as well. My dream of reuniting after so many years seemed like it just might come true, and Angela's revelation was another sign that it was time.

"I spoke to her last night so there's no way . . ." I said to my mom. "Why are you saying this to me?"

"Colleen called us because your cell phone's off," said my father. "It's true, Jimmy . . . she was killed last night. All we know is that someone broke into the apartment and that she's dead. That's all Colleen told us."

Linda's older sister Colleen never stopped treating me like I was part of the family. It was my friendship with her that ultimately led me to Linda, the woman who changed my life. The same was true for my family. My mother never stopped her persistent demand that Linda and I work things out and get back together. Even as years, and then a full decade, passed and the divorce was final, she told everyone that Linda would always be her daughter-in-law and that it was about time everyone else got wise and worked things out. It was one of those rare situations where no one wanted to believe the immediate evidence and held firm to the vision that love would someday win out over all those immature decisions we made in our youth. It kept the dream alive for me as well.

I sat up in the bed and rubbed my eyes, hoping I would open them and find that my parents weren't really there. That was when I began seriously considering the possibility that I wasn't asleep and that I really was lying in bed in my brother's spare room, and that what my parents were telling me might actually be true. I felt a terrible weight fill my chest and push me back toward the mattress as the thought entered my mind. A strange sensation began washing through me like the waves of a powerful ocean making it difficult to sit straight again. When I finally regained my balance and turned to put my feet on the bed, my mother took a step toward me and sat down.

"Where's Angela?" she asked in a low voice. "I didn't see her in the other room."

"She's in the basement on the couch," I said, and for the first time my mind went to her, completely unaware that everything in her world had just changed. "She slept downstairs because . . . I really don't know why. I need to go wake her up."

"Just wait," she said. "There's no need to rush that. Just let her sleep. She'll find out soon enough."

My brother came into the room, fully dressed and looking like he had been up much longer than I had been. "I just checked the Internet," he said. "It looks like there are some reports about what happened."

"I want to see them," I said as I jumped out of bed and ran into the other room. It was my last hope that there had been some great error and she was fine, or even in a hospital terribly wounded but alive. I sat down and looked at the page he had already brought up on the screen. It was a website from a local Chicago television station and the top headline confirmed my worst fear:

Woman Found Stabbed to Death in Evanston Apartment

Kenny clicked on the icon, and a video report began to load from the previous evening's newscast:

"Neighbors are stunned tonight as a woman is murdered in the north suburbs. Tonight police are searching for suspects. Linda Twyman was 43 years old and neighbors said she was screaming for her life . . ."

I fell to my knees and the room felt as if it caved in around me. There was no chance I was dreaming, no chance that it was a big mistake and that Linda was safe in bed or on her way to work, and no chance that I would ever see her alive again. The news report was like a giant nail being pounded into a wooden board that began splintering apart from the force. It felt like my life was splintering in all directions and there was nothing I could do to stop it. My parents came into the room and I could feel their hands on my back, hoping there was something they could do or say to ease the inevitable collapse. My hand reached blindly forward and grabbed hold of the chair, then pulled myself up to a standing position.

"I have to tell Angela," I said as I tried to compose myself. "She needs to know."

No one said anything to me as I walked down to the first floor, then opened the door to the basement. My adrenaline was pumping through my body, filling me with deceptive energy, as if I was about to run a race or walk onstage. I thought about how inappropriate that felt given what I was about to do. As I came to the bottom of the stairs, I could see Angela on the couch buried beneath two blankets. Part of me wanted to let her sleep and never tell her what I knew I couldn't avoid. The other adrenaline-soaked part wanted me to jump forward to get it over with, as if expediency would somehow soften the blow. I walked over and put my hand on her shoulder.

"Honey, wake up . . . I have something I have to tell you."

She looked up and saw the steady stream of tears pouring from my eyes.

CHAPTER FOUR

The next several days were a blur of activity and breakdowns. While I dove headfirst into my grief, Angela had a very different response. It was a week before her twentieth birthday, and the idea of losing her mother at such a young age, and in such a senseless manner, forced her into an emotional coma where feelings went to die. She was protecting herself, like a natural reflex that protects an injured hand or arm, or the memory of being burned by the hot surface of the electric stove that leaves an indelible mark upon one's consciousness, making all cooking devices seem suspect. Her friends gathered around her for support, and Angela did everything she could to make everything seem normal and undisturbed even though she was being cooked from the inside out. She displayed as little of the burn as possible, hoping that ignoring what happened would make it all go away.

I asked a friend in the far northern suburbs of Chicago to let us stay for the first few days, hoping the distance would insulate us from the details of the tragedy. The idea of seeing the apartment building or even stepping foot in Evanston was almost unbearable. Angela's best friend from

Oregon, Heather, flew in and met us at O'Hare; and Leslie, her best friend since high school, soon joined us at the house. Two of my best friends, Sharon Williams, who had worked with me for many years; and Neale Donald Walsch, would fly in from Oregon the next day to add support. Neale is the author of the *Conversations with God* series of books, and I knew his wisdom and energy would be an enormous help to all of us. We gathered our friends around us like barricades to hold us together and deflect the dark clouds that threatened to overwhelm the last remnants of our composure, but no matter who was there and what was said, the clouds became more ominous and terrifying with each passing moment. There was nothing we could do but stand still and let the wind whip us in whichever direction it wanted.

The first night together was the most tenuous. No one knew how to act or what to say, not sure if it was best to dive into the heart of the hurricane or stand at the edge and watch it uproot trees and destroy unsecured buildings at will. We bought wine and Chinese take-out, then gathered in the dark living room, huddling together as anyone would when the foundations of a house begin rattling from the stress of a storm. Someone started to recall funny stories from Linda's life and remember all the ways she touched and loved us. Angela joined in the discussion but seemed insulated from the real reason we were there. Regardless of the stories we told and the number of times we laughed, it didn't remove the cold fact that she was gone, and there was no bringing her back.

I was sitting just off to the side watching the girls, and regardless of whether any of us was dealing with the loss in the best way or not, it felt good to laugh and remember

Linda for the joyful presence she always radiated. She was the type of person everyone loved, as she walked through life with such a simple grace and gentle power. She was never loud or overbearing, preferring to remain in the background rather than shine on her own, but she also possessed an elegance that was unmistakable and rare, and she was the easiest person in the world to fall in love with. I knew this firsthand. Linda was my first love, and at least until then, the only woman I had felt called to give myself to fully and without reservations. The fact that I was young and naïve when we met, completely incapable of demonstrating the depths of my devotion, never diminished this fact. Every year or two I made a desperate plea to save the marriage, but Linda couldn't seem to let go of the betrayal she felt. I knew I would keep trying and would never fully accept failure until, of course, this latest tragic event brought a final end to all of my dreams.

My cell phone had only one picture of Linda stored in its memory, which I had taken a couple years earlier while she stood outside her apartment door. I looked at it several times that day, as if it was a final lifeline that led back to a time when anything was still possible. Long conversations with friends and relatives offering their love and support had drained the phone's battery, and the periodic beep alerted me that it was about to shut down on its own if I didn't turn it off myself. The sound was becoming annoying, so I reached into my pocket and took it out, then pressed the power button just as I had done a hundred times before. It had never deviated from its predictable pattern before—closing the various programs before finally going dark. I was startled by the fact that something very different was happening this time, something that I had never seen before.

The single picture of Linda that was stored on the phone flashed full screen and froze. No matter what I did after that, no matter what button I pushed, it would not leave but remained there as if unaffected by normal laws. I caught my breath and told the girls what had happened. At first they thought I was making it up, but then they saw the look in my eyes and knew it was real. They gathered around me to see the picture and to wonder what it meant. It was finally Heather who broke the silence.

"Oh my God," she said in a deep voice. "I'm feeling something that I've never felt before." We all turned around and looked at her. "I feel as if someone is standing right behind me, even though I know there isn't anyone there. I know it's her because it feels the same as every time I ever saw her. She's here with us right now . . . I know she is. I can almost feel her hand on my shoulder."

"Are you telling the truth?" Angela asked as tears finally began filling her eyes. "Don't just say that if it's not true. I need to know she's really here."

"I can feel her, too," Leslie said. "I know what Linda feels like, and she's in the room."

I knew they were right, though my eyes were still fixed on the phone that seemed to be alive and thinking on its own. I had heard that spirits are sometimes able to affect electrical objects, as if they're made of more than just physical atoms and cells. As I stared at the picture, I could almost sense her presence, as if she was telling us that she was still here and that we shouldn't worry about her.

Angela's voice filled with emotion. She looked into the air and said: "Mom, if you're here I need you to know something. I love you and I'm sorry." She collapsed onto the floor, and her friends wrapped their arms around her quaking body. The electricity in the air seemed to increase, making my skin tingle from the unseen force. I couldn't take my eyes off the camera, until suddenly, as if the spell was suddenly broken, the battery died and the screen went dark.

"I'm so sorry," Angela's muffled voice cried.

CHAPTER FIVE

We had to get out of Chicago as quickly as possible. The wake, funeral, and almost daily meetings with the police were beginning to take a toll on us all, and if it went on much longer I was afraid Angela wouldn't make it. From the morning my parents walked into my bedroom a week earlier with eyes that spoke of tragedy and terror to the moment we were exiting the city heading west, everything had changed. I was the one who had to wake up our daughter and tell her that she would never see her mother again, and I was also the one who had to play the role of ex-husband, standing somewhere between the past and the present, the one person who might not be as affected by the loss. How could anyone have known that my life felt like it had ended along with hers? It didn't feel like I had lost an ex-wife, but the woman I had been in love with for over twenty years. I felt like the future had been snatched from my hands as well—the possibility that my dream would finally be realized, that we might one day be reunited. All of that was gone now, and I couldn't stand to be in the city that had taken her life from us.

The police told us so little, saying that they couldn't disrupt the investigation by giving out too many details. All we knew was that two men were seen running out of the apartment Linda shared with Angela, and that when the police responded to the 911 call, they found her in Angela's bedroom. There was no forced entry, no sign of sexual assault, and nothing seemed to be missing. It was a mystery, and preliminary reports said that they weren't likely to find much forensic evidence. A special task force had been assigned to the case, one that had never left a murder unsolved, but after a week there was little reason to be optimistic. There was no obvious motive, and there didn't seem to be any connection between the murder and anyone Linda or Angela knew. After only a week it seemed the investigation had hit a dead end, and I didn't want to continue being torn apart by the tornado. That's why we decided to leave.

Instead of flying back to Oregon, I decided to buy a used BMW and drive. I needed a new car, and it seemed like a good way to decompress, allowing our minds to relax and unwind before the unimaginable task of re-entering normal life again. In truth, nothing would ever be normal again, and we all knew it. Our lives would be forever infused with the realization that no matter what adventures we had from that point on, Linda wouldn't be there to enjoy them with us. She was not moving to Oregon as we discussed; Linda and I would never be reunited, and Angela had lost her mother. There was no silver lining on the dark cloud that hung over our heads, and we all knew that whether we drove, took a train, or flew back to Oregon, we weren't going to outrun it.

I packed the car while Angela said goodbye to her friends, trying to arrange as many of her possessions as I could while still allowing room for three passengers. Heather would drive back with us, and I was happy to have her company. When the luggage was finally packed, I prepared to place the last and most important item—Linda's ashes—in the safest place I could find. The plastic urn was enclosed in a brown box that had been sealed for travel, but I felt I could still sense her energy seeping through and up my arms. I closed my eyes and could almost feel her there, as if she was reaching out to me or trying to communicate something that was critical for me to hear. I closed my eyes and listened, hoping I would be able to sense the message, or whatever it was she seemed to be stretching to convey. Then I felt a slight breeze caress my face, and with it the energy dissipated. I waited a few seconds to see if it would return again, hoping it was more than my imagination. When it didn't, I returned to my packing and fit the box between two of the suitcases, knowing it would be safe.

Angela, Heather, and I left Chicago late on the evening of December 5, the day before Angela's twentieth birthday. In the trunk were the gifts Linda had hidden in her bedroom closet, gifts Angela would now have to receive from a mother who wasn't there. We stopped and found a hotel just after midnight and prepared for the moment I dreaded more than her wake, more than her funeral, and more than the afternoon I had to go to the apartment and see her bloodstain on the floor. Angela and Heather seemed to have found a way to hold the terrible reality at arm's length, showing none of the emotions I knew were tearing their insides apart. One package held an inexpensive video camera, another some clothes that didn't seem to match

Angela's morphing style. Then there was the card written in such a familiar hand, round and open letters that seemed to match the spaciousness of her heart. Angela read the words out loud with the same cadence and emotion she would have used if the card had arrived when she was back in Oregon and Linda was safe in Evanston.

"Honey . . . I can't believe twenty years have already passed since you came into the world. You've made me so proud and I want you to know how much I love you and how happy I am to see the young woman you've turned into. Just don't forget that you'll always be my little girl, no matter what. I'll always be here for you. Mom."

Those last words fell to the floor like lead weights, but no sound came when they hit, only the cold silence that engulfed all three of us. If only I had read the card before she did then I could have hidden it so she would never see that last sentence. Linda wouldn't be able to keep her promise, through no fault of her own. Two nameless men with hoods pulled over their heads had stolen decades from her, years that had such promise and hope, and now her daughter stood in a small hotel room holding the card she had written only days earlier, a birthday present marking the twentieth year of her young life. Linda would not always be there, and there was nothing any of us could do to change that terrible fact.

After three days of driving, we were ready to be home. We had crossed through the Rocky Mountains and were getting closer to Oregon with every mile. If we stayed on I-80 until we reached Sacramento, then cut up I-5 into Oregon, it would take another day and a half. Emotions were frayed and the girls were becoming more and more restless. If there was a way to speed along the journey, then I was willing to consider it.

"There's a highway that cuts off from this little town in Nevada called Winnemucca that would take a lot of time off the trip," Heather said as she looked at the map. "We might even be able to make it back to Ashland tonight if we take Route 140."

I was driving and couldn't look at the map, but smaller highways that cut through steep mountain ranges never felt like a good bet, especially in December.

"I don't know if that's a good idea, Heather. The highway might even be closed. Are there any towns on the road?"

"Between Winnemucca and Lakeview . . . no, not really." Heather did a quick calculation to determine how far we would have to travel without the aid of gas stations and hotels. "It looks like it might be 200 miles till we get to Lakeview. I say we pull over and ask what the road's like. If it's fine, I think we should take it."

"I agree with Heather," Angela said. They were both in the backseat and seemed to have made up their minds. "I can't stand being in this car any longer. If we can get back tonight, then I say we do it."

I pulled into a gas station in Winnemucca and decided to ask around to see if Highway 140 was open. I also wanted to make sure there were no imminent snowstorms on the way. The last place I wanted to be was on a mountain pass in the middle of a blizzard. Everything I learned seemed to indicate that the road was safe, and there didn't seem to be any bad weather on the horizon. Deciding to go against a strong intuition that told me I was making the wrong choice, we chose to take the shortcut.

The highway seemed fine for the first seventy-five or so miles. The pavement was dry, and though there was not much traffic that passed us, an occasional truck coming from the opposite direction told me that traffic was moving both ways. Then we came to the area I was most concerned about, the stretch that seemed to hug the side of the mountain with very little room for error. I was surprised to see that there were no guardrails keeping cars from rolling over the edge, but at least the weather was still cooperating.

Then everything changed.

The snow began to fall lightly at first, just enough to fill my heart with nervousness, but within minutes it had escalated to a winter storm. The wipers were moving at full speed, but they were no match for the huge flakes that were piling up outside. Neither Angela nor Heather seemed to understand the seriousness of the situation and were making small talk in the back seat, while my hands were glued to the steering wheel with my eyes open as wide as I could get them. I was driving no more than twenty miles per hour, and on the rare occasion that a truck passed us, I braced for possible disaster. I finally called for silence in the car, and for the first time the girls realized that something was wrong.

"Why are you so stressed?" Angela asked. "You've driven in snow lots of times."

"But not on the edge of a cliff," I said, without moving my eyes away from the windshield. "I don't know if you noticed this or not, but there isn't a guardrail on the other side of the road. If we were to slide even a few feet, we would fall to the bottom. I'm not going to allow another tragedy tonight."

From that moment on, there was silence in the car. Angela and Heather realized the possible consequences to us leaving the interstate, but now it was just as dangerous to go back as it was to go forward. The rate of the snowfall was increasing with each minute, and the frequency of passing cars and trucks decreased to nothing. Was it possible that the road ahead was closed, or that it was even worse the farther we went? I knew that my options were limited. If I stopped along the narrow road, we were subject to being hit by a vehicle that didn't see us in time. I also hadn't noticed any turnoffs or exits, and we still had to travel at least fifty miles before we hit Lakeview. There didn't seem to be any choice but to keep moving forward at the slowest pace possible.

That's when it happened. It was the kind of thing that could occur while driving down any country road, and my reaction was automatic. A rabbit darted in front of the car, moving from the outside lane directly into the headlights of the BMW, and I instinctively swerved slightly to the left. It happened so fast that my mind was unable to process the risk I had just taken. If the road had been dry it would have hardly mattered, but with the snow and slick pavement, a very different outcome quickly developed. The car slid instead of recovering back to the right. I knew that touching the brake would be disastrous, so I tried to readjust by steering toward the lane I belonged in. I've heard that time slows down when confronted with imminent disaster, and for the first time I discovered that the stories are true. Nothing mattered but avoiding the edge of the cliff that was approaching faster and with little chance of recovery. I had no choice but to brake and pray that the slower speed would save us. The girls closed their eyes, sensing what was happening, and for a second I considered the irony of the situation. We were about to die and join Linda, and there was nothing I could do but wait and hope.

The car finally slowed to a stop, and I felt the front left tire shudder against the loose gravel that led to the open air and certain death. We held our breath, hoping that it would make a difference, and seconds later, without thinking, I put the car in reverse and found solid ground once again. We were alone on the snow-covered highway and realized with amazing clarity just how close we had come to losing our lives. I don't know how long we sat there, but it was long enough for me to remember every detail of the road, the cliff, and the terrible fear I experienced as I wondered if we would ever make it to Oregon.

CHAPTER SIX

It was a month after Linda's death and I was at Neale's house in Ashland celebrating his son's birthday. Most of our friends were gathered on the main floor, talking in small groups, interacting as we always had. I tried to pull myself together, to laugh and celebrate with the others, but the crushing weight of Linda's death was pressing hard against me, and I decided to escape to the basement where I knew I could be alone for a few minutes. Neale must have seen me leave and followed a minute or so later.

"How are you doing, buddy?" he asked in a quiet voice. "Don't feel like you need to stay and pretend everything's all right. Everyone knows what you're going through and would understand if you're not ready for this kind of thing."

"It's fine," I said as I sat down on the couch. "I just needed to be alone and get my head together. It's a bit overwhelming, but at the same time this is my family. I'm not going to heal this by hiding away in my house."

"And your family understands," he said as he sat down next to me. "Everyone's here for you in whatever way you need to help you get over this."

There was something about the way he said the words

"help you get over this" that caused a strange reaction inside me. I didn't want to ever get over it, and that fact was only then becoming conscious in my mind. It felt as if my grief kept me connected to Linda, as if the intensity of the emotion connected me to the place where she now existed and lived. Who would I be if I no longer felt sad or if the power of the loss receded in my memory?

"I appreciate that," I finally said to him, "but this really isn't the kind of thing you ever really get over."

Neale leaned forward and looked into my eyes. We had been friends long enough for me to know when he was about to say something profound, something that would likely influence me in ways I would discover only with the passing of time. I braced myself for the impact.

"That's true," he said. "You'll never get over this, but there will come a day when it's no longer over *you*. It's like being in Oregon during the winter . . . the clouds are almost always there and you feel their oppressive weight even when you're not thinking about them. Then the day comes when the clouds part and everything changes. You remember winter and can even conjure up the feelings if you want, but you don't sense them in the same way. It may take a while, but one day when you're not thinking about it you'll realize the clouds are gone, and then you'll know what I mean."

Three years later that day finally came. Until then Linda's death had been like a dark cloud hanging over my life and I felt it pushing down on me even when I wasn't consciously aware of it. I still missed her and wished she was there, but the sadness had suddenly shifted. If I focused hard enough and tried to pull up images of Linda, I could summon those familiar feelings, but otherwise they were replaced by a dull void that had become an accepted part of my very being. I realized that I was sad about no longer being sad. There was a strange comfort the sadness had brought, as if it made me feel closer to Linda or as if I wasn't honoring her if I actually felt resolved. I wanted to be sad and when I realized I wasn't, it was like I'd lost a friend.

The investigation into Linda's murder hadn't moved forward at all, at least as far as we knew. Television programs like *CSI* make us believe that forensic results are almost instantaneous and lead to the arrest of the guilty suspect in an hour or less. That illusion couldn't have been further from the truth. Though the detectives were still as tightlipped as they had always been about the details of the case, I discovered that it took over six months for the forensic evidence to return, and even then it was limited and inconclusive. Extensive interviews with everyone even remotely involved in Linda's life also failed to turn up any hopeful leads, and as far as anyone could tell, it was falling farther and farther back on the backlog of active cases.

Then one day, all of that changed.

I was in North Carolina leading a retreat when I heard that a new lead had developed, giving the police hope that they might finally solve the case, and yet the fact that I discovered the information almost by accident, in an e-mail from Linda's friend Gina, made me wonder why I was being kept in the dark. Gina had done more to keep everyone focused on solving the murder than anyone else. Her constant badgering of the police led to us learning more details than they wanted us to, and the many prayer vigils she helped organize at Linda's apartment over the years kept hope alive. I was checking my e-mails after lunch when I came across a letter she forwarded to me about some people who were trying to get Linda's story on *America's Most Wanted*. At first I wasn't particularly interested in the idea, but as I read further, something caught my attention.

"Detective Glue thinks it's a bad idea since he already has someone who confessed, and he doesn't want anything to get in the way of the new investigation."

Confessed? To read those words written in such a matter was like a blow to my gut. Why hadn't anyone told us that there was a new lead . . . even more, that someone had actually confessed to the murder? I went through the chain of e-mails and learned a bit more. There was apparently a man in custody in a prison near Chicago who one day decided to come clean and admitted to killing a young woman in Evanston three years earlier. Everything he told them matched the details of Linda's murder, leading them to believe that they had one of the two killers. The fact that he had already been convicted of at least one other murder meant that they could take their time gathering more evidence before filing charges. In other words, he wasn't going anywhere, so why rush? Better to have everything in order and make a strong case than act too quickly and risk everything.

But why hadn't anyone shared this information with me, or even more important, with Angela? She was just beginning to recover from the blow of losing her mother and had recently been promoted to weekend manager at the LA Fitness health club where she worked. Even *I* wondered if it was a good idea to tell her when formal charges had yet to be filed. What if it was just another false lead and ended up being a narcissistic criminal wanting some attention and an occasional free sandwich? Judging from my own response to the news, I began to understand the wisdom of holding off for the time being. It stirred up all the emotions that had just begun to settle, and I found myself swimming in a sea filled with turbulent waves and dark shadows once again.

Trying to lead a retreat while processing these emotions was almost impossible. I had no choice but to share with the group what was happening, and they, of course, became my strongest supporters. There were others in the room who had recently lost loved ones, so we used the emotions to help us all heal on deep levels. It ended up being a gift, but that didn't diminish the fact that I was now back where I started. The grief I thought I had healed was back once again.

The night after I read Gina's e-mail was the most difficult for me since that first week. In the rare moments when I did drift off to sleep, my mind was filled with dreams of snowstorms and cliffs, terror and death. When I woke up the next morning, I tried to shake off the images, but they were more persistent than I thought. I could literally feel the sensation of the car sliding helplessly toward the edge of the cliff then falling hundreds of feet to the valley floor. It was like a waking dream that invaded my mind whenever I held still or let my brain relax. In one dream the car would teeter at the edge, but then we would back up and safely escape. In another, all three of us died when the car crashed at the bottom. I didn't tell anyone about these visions because I was starting to worry myself. Was it the result of the stress I was feeling, or was it something deeper, even the beginning of a final mental split that had been narrowly averted before but which was now suddenly imminent?

I flew home after the retreat and tried to return to normal. My concern about the sadness disappearing was no longer an issue since it felt as strong as it ever had before. Then there was the question of how and when I should tell Angela. Part of me understood the reason for not letting her know earlier, at least until the police were sure they had the right man. At the same time, I wanted to make sure she heard it when she had time to process the new development. With her new position and the stress of working fifty or more hours a week, I knew she needed room to feel the impending grief just as I did. I decided to take her out to dinner on Monday evening, and since she had the next two days off, I would likely break the news to her then.

We were sitting on the patio of a local restaurant and had just finished our first drink. The entrées would arrive soon. I decided it was the right moment. I sat forward in my chair and set my glass of wine down on the table.

"There's something I need to tell you that I learned about a week ago," I said. "It wasn't easy for me to hear, and it won't be easy for you either." I nervously picked up the glass again and took a sip of my wine before continuing. "It looks like someone confessed to killing your mom. He hasn't been charged yet because they want to make sure that they have enough evidence to convict him. The good thing is that he's already in jail, so they know where to find him. He's not leaving."

Here eyes grew heavy and dark. "When did this happen?" she asked, trying to hide her shock.

"I don't know," I told her. "I think it may have happened

awhile ago, but it's the first I've heard about it. I never thought they were going to tell me much, but I'm surprised they didn't tell *you*. I found out through an e-mail Gina sent. It was mentioned, but not in detail."

"Gina knew but no one told me?" she said, growing even more agitated. "The detective told me he would tell me what was happening even if it wasn't good. I'm really mad they kept this from me."

"They did it because no one wants you to go through all this until they know they have the right man. There are a few details the police never told anyone else about the case that are only known by the killers. If this guy were to ever mention them, then it would be over. But he hasn't yet. I was told that he did admit to other things that led the investigators to believe he's telling the truth, but they can't take the chance of him recanting his confession if they don't have all the evidence first."

"I don't care," she said as tears began flowing down her face. "They still should have told me. I have a right to know."

"Yes, you do. That's why I'm telling you now. I knew it would be hard because of how it felt for me when I heard. It stirred everything up again, all the emotions I thought were healed and then suddenly there they were again. But at least there's movement . . . finally. I was starting to think that this would never be solved."

"Where's the other person?" she asked. "There were two men."

"He apparently admitted that he had a partner, but hasn't given him up yet. All we can do is hope."

"I'm tired of hoping," Angela said. "I don't want to hope anymore. I just want this whole thing to be over."

CHAPTER SEVEN

We all wanted it to be over, and I wanted the dreams of driving over the edge of the cliff to end as well. I was beginning to think that they were pushing me to the edge of insanity, and I knew I had to do something about it. Why had they suddenly surfaced in a way I couldn't explain or avoid? Angela's anger over not being told about the confession was understandable, but my obsession with an accident that hadn't even happened wasn't. One way or another I had to find resolution.

I have to go back, return to the cliff, and lay the whole thing to rest.

The thought seemed to come out of nowhere, and I resisted it for several days before considering it as a real alternative. What would going back accomplish, other than showing me just how close we had come to dying ourselves? There was a link there that I couldn't consciously identify, as if Linda's death and our near disaster were somehow related. It was obvious I wasn't going to discover the link by just dwelling on the subject, so without telling anyone where I was going, I got in my car and started driving, knowing that I was heading into the very heart of something I couldn't understand, and something I simply couldn't avoid.

What would I do once I arrived? It was a question I had no answer to, and I knew I wouldn't have an answer until the actual moment I stood looking over the edge of the cliff. I saw myself doing just that in numerous dreams, as if there was something waiting for me at the bottom. I saw myself standing there on the pavement, looking over the precipice with a deep sense of peace and completion. All I knew for sure was that I couldn't wait and theorize any longer. One way or another I needed to resolve my feelings, and that wasn't going to happen until I arrived.

Two days later I was pulling into Lakeview looking for a hotel to spend the night. That was when I spotted the Budget Inn, the hotel where Angela, Heather, and I had spent the night three and a half years earlier. Being a creature of habit and perhaps even superstition, I pulled into the parking lot and went inside. I could see the figure of a large, muscular man in the office with his back turned toward me. I cleared my throat to let him know I was there, though I knew it wasn't necessary. The massive Native American stood up and turned toward me.

Victor!

The dream of sliding toward the edge of the cliff saturated my mind while I slept that night. It showed up in a wide variety of ways throughout the night, sometimes in strange combinations. In one dream I was at my childhood home in New York getting ready to go to school. My mother decided to let me drive, even though I was only twelve, and as soon as we got away from the house I was back on that terrible highway with the blizzard and the suicidal rabbit.

My mother screamed as I hit the brakes, and we slid over the edge to our death. In another I was with Linda and a two-year-old Angela driving somewhere I didn't recognize. It seemed to be the desert with a flat, dry landscape. The snow never materialized, but I did lose control, and slid toward the edge of the Grand Canyon. Luckily in that dream we all survived.

I left my room at the Budget Inn early the next morning wondering if I would see Victor at the front desk and, most important, if he would try to talk me out of going back to the cliff. The sensation that I was being watched as I walked toward my car was hard to shake, as if someone, or even the cliff itself, knew I was on the way. I walked into the office to drop off the key and saw a small middle-aged woman with red hair behind the counter. She smiled as I entered.

"Good morning . . . dropping off the key?"

"Yes, I am," I said, looking around the room. "The man who was here last night, Victor . . . is he still around by any chance?"

"Sorry, but Victor left at six . . . that's when I arrived. But wait a minute . . . you were in room twenty-three, right? He told me I was supposed to give you this if I saw you."

She held out a small piece of paper folded in half. I reached across the counter and took the sheet, then took several steps toward the door before opening the note. His handwriting was neat, with small rounded letters, which surprised me given the size of his enormous hands. I took a deep breath before I let my mind settle on the message he left.

If you get this letter then you're probably on your way to the highway. That means you didn't take my advice not to continue, so

I hope you'll consider what I'm about to tell you now. This is not meant to scare you, but to open your eyes and help keep them open. If you do choose to go you'll need to remember two things. The first is that sometimes things you perceive with your eyes are not always what they appear to be. This is doubly true of the area you're traveling to now. The second is that regardless of what happens, you'll be fine. What do I mean by this? That's what you'll have to discover for yourself. No matter what happens, remember these two things I've written. Victor

I swallowed hard, then folded the note and put it back in my pocket.

"Have a good trip," the woman from behind the counter said.

"Thanks . . . I'll try."

As I opened the car door, I remembered the conversation I'd had with Neale days earlier when I began the journey back to the cliff. He was the only friend I felt comfortable talking to about the obsession since he had been with me from the very beginning, and his wisdom had already served me well in many ways. Since I was beginning the journey from my new home in Portland, I had to stop in Ashland and call to make sure he was home.

"There's obviously a reason for the vision," he said as we sat in his kitchen. "Something like that doesn't keep showing up unless there's something we need to learn, or there's something connected to it."

"But what could I possibly have to learn from that?" I asked him. "We almost died, which would have made a tragic situation infinitely worse. Maybe I feel guilty for deciding to take that highway in the first place. I should have known better and should have decided to stay on the interstate. To think that I put us at so much risk . . ."

"That's possible, but I have the feeling that there's something more. What does that spot represent to you?"

"I guess it represents how easily things can happen, and how quickly we can go from just driving down the road to something that changes us forever."

"Which is what happened to Linda," he continued. "She had no idea something like that was going to happen to her, even ten minutes before it did. She was probably in her apartment cleaning up or getting her clothes ready for work the next day. Life can be that uncertain, and you experienced that when you almost went over the cliff."

"That's all true," I said, "but I also have the feeling that there's something more. It's like the place is calling me, as if I need to go back for something."

"Why would you need to go back there?"

"I have no idea, but I feel like Richard Dreyfus's character in *Close Encounters*. He became obsessed with the mountain because he was being called to go there. Maybe I'm being called back to the same mountain pass where we almost died. What if something's supposed to happen there?"

"What could possibly need to happen?"

"I don't know, Neale, but I can't get it out of my mind."

"Then follow it and see where it leads," he said. "I think you should do whatever you think is going to give you some kind of closure. This may sound harsher than it's intended to sound, but three and a half years have passed since Linda was killed. Don't you think she would want you to move on?"

"I just have this feeling that I won't be able to do that

until I go back. Something's waiting for me, either at the cliff or . . . I don't even know . . . I just know I need to see it again, then maybe it will all be over."

The time passed quickly as I drove, and I was almost surprised when I began entering into the most treacherous area, not far from the spot I had every confidence of finding. The steep-sided, sharp-crested ridges spotted with juniper trees are among of the most rugged in the area. Deep V-shaped valleys shot off from the cliffs far below, and I began to see just how easy it would be to plummet to the bottom. Most stretches of the road have no guardrails, meaning that a single mishap would be disastrous. It was one thing to sense this in the midst of a dark, blinding snowstorm, but seeing it in the light of day was something much more terrifying. Elevations ranged anywhere from 4,000 feet to the high point of Parrot Peak at 8,400. It was stunning and dangerous, and I sensed that I was moving straight into the heart of a dark mystery.

I found a spot that seemed familiar around 3 PM. Though it had been dark when I'd been there three and a half years earlier, there were several markers that were fixed permanently in my mind, and I was sure that if I found an area where all three were present, it would be the spot I was searching for. The first marker was a sharp, ninety-degree turn to the right, which meant I was looking for one going to the left since I was coming in from the opposite direction. Next, I remembered seeing a sign for a scenic turnoff about a half mile before the rabbit ran in front of us, and then saw a rest area that fit that description down the road. Finally, there was the spot itself, with its loose gravel and sheer drop-off, just inches from the side of the road. I pulled the car over, nearly certain that it was the place. I felt a strange tension run through my body as I opened the door and stood up.

I was driving the red Toyota Prius I'd bought a year and a half earlier when I traded in the BMW. I looked around and felt sure that everything matched, then stepped to the side of the cliff to survey the distance we would have plunged to if we hadn't stopped in time. It was at least 150 feet straight down, leaving no doubt we would have all perished. I was also struck by the stunning panoramic view, with high peaks and rugged terrain in the distance, none of which I would have seen on the last trip. The trees thickened at the bottom of the cliff, and the prospect of anyone ever finding us if we had gone over seemed remote.

And that's when I saw it. It was hard to tell from the road, but I was sure I saw a car hidden in the trees below, a silver car, the same color as the one I was driving at the time. It was on its side, and from that distance I could see that it was terribly wrecked. The angle made it impossible to see the make or model. Was it a BMW? There was no way to know, but I was relatively sure it was. What were the odds that another silver BMW had plummeted over the exact same cliff and rested there as forgotten as mine would have been? I felt the hair on the back of my neck stand up and experienced a mild episode of vertigo. Steadying myself, I took a step backward.

I had to know. I remembered everything Victor had told me, but I had come so far and the mystery had suddenly taken an unexpected turn. I got back in the Prius and drove to the turn-off half a mile away, grabbed my bottle of water, then walked back. It was a sunny, warm day and there were still several hours of sunlight left. If I could find a path or an easy way down the cliff, I would hopefully be able to find the car. For some reason I had the feeling that that was the place to start, though I had no idea what would come next.

I arrived back at the precipice ten minutes later and surveyed the land below. There was no possibility of climbing down the steep cliff where I stood, and there was no obvious path anywhere in the vicinity. I walked a half mile or so down the road until the decline softened, and I thought I could make it safely down to the valley below. There were not as many trees to brace myself against as I had hoped, but the combination of sliding and stumbling seemed to be working. It took at least fifteen minutes to reach the bottom, then I began winding my way over to the spot where I remembered seeing the car.

The trees grew much thicker the farther I went, and it was hard to tell for certain if I was heading in the right direction. The sharp rocks were also becoming a much more formidable adversary. One slip and I stood the risk of being badly injured, and if that happened then it would be a very long time before anyone stumbled across me. I could die here, after all, I thought, and that was something I couldn't let happen.

Then I saw the sun reflect off a metal surface in the distance. As I walked closer I realized I had found the wrecked car and that it was much more badly damaged than I first thought. I climbed over broken trees and other debris that had fallen prey to the plummeting wreck until I stood next to it. Within seconds I realized I was right; though difficult to see many details, it was definitely a silver BMW, the same model as my own. I was standing at the side of the car and felt my heart begin to race as I walked around to see the license plate. What was I expecting to find—that it really was my car and that I actually had died that night? Was I reliving *The Sixth Sense,* where a man discovers he's really dead and only thinks he's alive? Of course the idea was ludicrous, but I was still deathly afraid to look.

The license plates were gone. Why someone would choose to go to this extent and remove them was beyond me, but since I didn't find a skeleton inside the vehicle, the possibility did exist. It was more likely that a salvage crew had come to remove the dead bodies and the plates but decided that pulling the car up would take too much effort. They probably decided to leave it where it was, figuring that no one would ever be peering over the edge, and certainly no one would be foolish enough to hike to the spot. Why would they, unless they themselves had nearly died on the exact same cliff while driving a car that was an exact replica of this one? Nothing would have stopped that person from risking everything to see for himself what happened, adding more mystery to an already impossible situation.

I must have stood there looking at the car for an hour, going through the front seat and glove compartment expecting to find something that belonged to me. I didn't. Then I searched the area for anything that would tell me it was all a coincidence and that it was time to leave it all behind and go back to Portland. Once again, I found nothing. Then I realized that the sun was going to begin setting behind the distant hills and the last thing I wanted was to try to make my way up the cliff in the dark. I took a deep breath and began winding my way back to the area safest to climb.

I had wandered at least a half mile looking for the

place I had originally climbed down, realizing that all other options were far too dangerous. I also realized that I was walking farther into the brush away from the cliff since it was so overgrown near its base. It wasn't much of a risk, but I decided to establish my position by focusing on the hills and where the sun was dipping toward the horizon. The last thing I wanted was to get lost and become a casualty of this strange place where, according to Victor, the spirits weren't so friendly.

I had been walking for about a half hour, definitely enough time to find the path back up the cliff. I tried to locate the hills I was using to reference my position but by then I was too deep in the forest to see them. The shadows were also starting to thicken, and I felt my anxiety begin to rise. I could hear the sound of running water nearby and decided that it might be my best hope. If I could find the stream and follow it back in the direction I knew the road to be, then it would surely lead me back to safety. It was a good theory, though in retrospect it made very little sense.

Minutes later I came to the stream and began following it to the right, back toward the cliff and my final release from this ridiculous adventure. But what would I do once I did find my way to the car and the road leading home? Did I even want to solve the mystery of the destroyed BMW at the bottom of the cliff, or was it better to leave it behind? Then I remembered that I should have written down the VIN, a simple piece of information that would have solved the dilemma. I could have easily called the DMV the next day and referenced the number, realizing to my profound relief that it had all been a coincidence. I thought about going back, but the risk was growing as the sun was setting. It was better to move on, find the path, and get back to the car. The clock was ticking faster and faster.

Half an hour passed, and I wasn't any closer to my goal. By then it was nearly dark and I began to panic. Luckily the temperature was warm enough that I would easily survive the night, so I convinced myself that the safest thing was to relax and get some rest. It was definitely a better idea than getting more lost or trying to climb to the road with no light. If I had known this was going to happen I would have brought a flashlight and better clothing. Luckily there was plenty of water, and once daylight hit I would be able to find my way back and get food. I took a deep breath and sat down with my back resting against a large tree. As long as I didn't encounter a mountain lion or a pack of hungry coyotes, I would be fine. After a while I closed my eyes.

CHAPTER EIGHT

A sound startled me from my rest and I sat straight up. Heavy, purposeful steps were moving in my direction. With supersonic ears turned in the direction of the noise, I listened for anything that might tell me whether I should relax or be afraid. The sound stopped for a moment, then started again. There definitely was someone, or something, coming toward me. Did they know I was there? Was it better to announce myself or lie low and hope they went away?

"Hello, is there anyone there?" I asked, deciding to make my presence known. Then I saw a flashlight point in my direction and heard the sound of a deep male voice.

"Yes . . . are you lost or just taking a rest?"

I could tell from the sound of this person's voice that I was safe. I'm not sure how I knew this, but there was something about his tone and the energy he emitted that told me everything was going to be okay.

"I'm lost," I said, standing up from the tree. "Thank God someone came . . . I thought I'd be here all night."

The silhouette of a tall man stepped out from a thick bunch of trees shining the flashlight on the ground in front of him. He looked to be around fifty or fifty-five years old, and though it was hard to tell too much in the dark with a flashlight pointed toward me, he seemed to possess a powerful presence. "Where is it you were trying to get to?" he asked. "I know you're not out for a camping trip. If you were, you'd probably have more than that water bottle."

I looked at the ground where the bottle was sitting. "No, not a camping trip. I was trying to get to the road where my car is parked and must have gotten turned around."

"Yes, you did. The road's about half a mile that way." It was only then that I saw him clearly, and he pointed in the opposite direction I had been walking. "If you kept going this way you would have never made it out. It gets more and more hairy the deeper into this forest you get."

"Then I'm grateful you came along to save me. My name is Jimmy." I held out my hand when he came close enough. Though the darkness made it difficult to see too many details, I noticed deep lines in his face that seemed to indicate one who was accustomed to a wilderness like this one, and yet I had to wonder why he was there at all. Perhaps he was hiking through the forest as I was, though he certainly knew the terrain far better. I considered the possibility that he was an inhabitant of the area, though I had seen no signs of houses or roads leading off the main highway. The cliff alone seemed to negate this possibility. Answers certainly weren't going to arrive on their own, and I had no choice but to wait and see where this new development would lead.

"I'm Richard," he said, offering his own hand. "I live down the creek a bit. I had a feeling that something was wrong. I guess it's a sense you develop when you've been living in the woods alone for a while."

"You live out here? I'm amazed . . . it seems so . . . harsh."

He smiled. "Well, there's a little community of people not far away, so I have plenty of company. We help each other out. That being said, I'm going to suggest you don't try to make it back to your car tonight. I can get you back to the cliff, but getting up in the dark is a different story. I wouldn't risk it if I were you. I have a cabin with a spare bedroom. Why don't you stay there for the night and I'll get you to your car in the morning."

I looked at Richard and wondered again if I should trust him. It seemed like solid advice, and a bedroom sounded much better than leaning against a hard tree. There was also something about his demeanor that made me trust him, as if I was perfectly safe in his care. If I had sensed any danger I would have gladly stayed where I was and waited for the sun to rise, but given the opportunity and his friendly manner, I decided to accept his invitation.

"That sounds like a great idea," I finally said. "If you don't mind, I would love to join you."

"Great, then follow me . . . it's not too far."

There was a small deer path running along the stream that was only visible with the flashlight, and Richard led the way. His steps were solid and sure, while mine were tentative. I was afraid of stepping wrong on a rock or getting caught on a tree trunk, but I soon realized that as long as I followed him I was perfectly safe. In the distance I saw a glowing light, then shortly after that the form of a small cabin came into view.

"That's it up there," he said. "It's not much, but I built it myself and live a pretty simple life."

"How long have you been out here?" I asked.

"Just about ten years now. It's hard to believe it's been that long, but it has. I'm from California originally . . . the Bay Area. I don't guess there are too many people who live as simply as I do anywhere, but I'm perfectly satisfied with it."

"You said that there's a community near here . . . so you're not alone."

"I'm definitely not alone," he said as he stopped and turned around. "Most of those here like to live out of the way, and this area fits the bill perfectly. As you've noticed, there are no roads to get back here and not even any utilities. Everything I have I had to either bring in or make myself. After ten years it's just become normal. I'm not sure I could go back to living like I once did."

"It's incredible," I said to him. "Lots of people dream of living off the land like that, but very few have the ability to do it."

"I can't say I had much ability when I first arrived, but over time I've developed the skill. That's how it is for all of us. In fact, there's a little party taking place tonight . . . a barn dance. It happens now and then . . . everyone from the community gets together to talk and hang out. There's a live band and plenty of dancing. I was going to go, but I don't have to if you would rather stay in the cabin and rest."

I almost felt that the comment was a test of some kind. He looked at me, waiting for an answer, as if it would tell him what kind of person I was. Was I adventurous enough to join him, or would I play it safe and wait for morning to arrive? The fact that I had come that far was enough to tell me that I wasn't the type to sit in a cabin when such an unusual opportunity awaited me.

"Of course you're more than welcome to join me if you want," he finally said when he realized I didn't know what to say. We were standing just outside the cabin and the light from the window was reflecting off Richard's face, giving him an angelic glow. The longer I was with him, the more comfortable I felt.

"I would love to go," I told him. "Why not . . . I may as well enjoy myself if I'm going to spend the night in the woods."

"I agree. Of course, you *could* just sit in my cabin by yourself if you want. I don't have anything to steal and there's no television. But I think you'll really like the dance. You'll probably find that the people you meet there are really fascinating."

We stepped into his cabin, which was tidy and neat, as well as extremely compact. Everything seemed to have a place, and there was no corner left unused. The main room was both sitting area and kitchen, and there were two doors on either side that I assumed were bedrooms.

"You'll be in that one over there," he said, pointing to the right. "Not much, but it's comfortable."

"Thank you," I answered. "You have no idea how grateful I am."

"Of course I do. I saw where you were sleeping, remember?"

"I suppose you did. Though I have to say that I've had worse. It's better than flying to Tokyo in the middle seat of a crowded airplane. That's a flight I'll never forget."

"Between two large men?" he asked.

"How did you know?" I said as I remembered the feeling of claustrophobia I'd experienced on the flight. "That's exactly how it was."

"You're a lot smaller than I am, but I've had the same thing happen . . . not to Tokyo, but to London. I used to travel a lot when I was a lawyer years ago. I think you can say that my life is the exact opposite of how it once was."

"I can see that. You weren't run out of town, were you? You know what they say about lawyers."

He smiled at the thought. "No, not run out of town, but in a way, yes. I guess you could say I ran myself out of town. I did everything I was supposed to do and had everything the world says is important, but I wasn't happy. I wasn't married and didn't have anything holding me there, so one day I got in my car and started driving. A few weeks later I ended up here."

"Along with the others," I said. "Once again, this whole thing amazes me."

"It's more amazing than you can imagine," he said in a way that sparked my curiosity. "You'll find that out a little later."

"What time does the dance start?" I asked, hoping to get a bit more information.

"It's already started," he said. "Since you don't have anything with you, you don't need to get ready. Why don't we head over there now?"

"I'll leave my water bottle." It was meant to be a joke, like leaving a suitcase which I didn't have. "How many people live out here? I didn't see any town on the atlas I bought."

"There are no towns, and as far as the number, that varies. Sometimes we'll have a hundred people at a party like this. We'll use any excuse to get together."

"What do people who live out here do? I'm assuming there are no stores or other signs of civilization."

"No stores, no factories, just really wonderful people who like their privacy."

My mind went to stories I'd heard about the illegal pot-growing operations that wilderness areas like this were famous for, especially in nearby California. I prepared myself for a barn full of hippies smoking dope trying to evade the law. The adventure was getting more exciting by the moment.

"You strike me as a very deep man," I said as we stepped out of the cabin, then onto the path heading the opposite direction we originally came.

"What makes you say that?" he asked as he looked over his shoulder.

"I don't exactly know," I said. "But you do seem thoughtful and deep. I guess living out here in the wilderness makes a person more introspective."

"That makes sense. I just try to stay in the moment, to tell you the truth. I think that's the key to life. Too many people live in the past or in the future, but they miss so much that way. The only thing we can ever really experience is right now . . . this very moment."

"Living in the past . . ." I said, feeling the impact of his words. "That sounds familiar."

"I have to ask, why are you out here? There aren't too many people who just happen to brave this area. It's pretty remote and not too friendly."

"I met a native man in Lakeview who said the same thing," I told him. "He said that there are things that happen out here that are pretty far out, maybe even negative. He also said that it was extremely sacred to his tribe at one point."

"Still is. Not sure about it being negative, though.

Energy is neither malignant nor benign . . . it simply reacts to what you bring to it. If you're positive and happy, then that's what you attract."

"So you believe that the area is unusual and even sacred?" I asked.

"I believe that unusual things happen out here . . . definitely. But I don't want to put a label on it. And you didn't answer my question: what brought you out here in the first place?"

I told him about Linda and the near accident we'd had while driving back to Oregon three years earlier. I also told him about the obsession I'd been experiencing that prompted this journey, leaving out the BMW I found at the bottom of the cliff.

"What do you think of all that?" I asked, half expecting him to think I was crazy.

"What do I think? Let's just say I'm not surprised. I'll leave it at that for now. I also have a feeling that you'll get a few answers at the party we're going to."

I could hear bluegrass music in the distance, then saw light glowing through the trees, which told me we were there. Everyone must have arrived before us since there was no one lingering outside the door. Nothing seemed out of the ordinary . . . in fact, I had the feeling I was welcome before I even arrived. There was nothing to account for that feeling, except, perhaps, the welcome I had already received from Richard.

"There it is," he said as he turned around and smiled. "Get ready for the time of your life."

He walked fast until he arrived at the barn, then waited for me to catch up. As if parting the curtains for the beginning of a play, he opened the door and let me step inside. The room was filled with people, some dancing and others lingering about in different groups chatting and drinking. They were not dressed in a manner that was consistent or distinct. In fact, I couldn't really define an overall style at all, as if they came from many different places and from many walks of life. Some were dressed in outfits that resembled my parents' square-dancing uniforms from when I was a child, others wore jeans and T-shirts, and a few were dressed as if they were going to a party much more exclusive than this one. Two or three of the older men saw us walk in and stepped up to shake Richard's hand.

"Good to see you, old boy," a large man with short silver hair said. "I see you brought a new friend."

"This is Jimmy," he said. "Believe it or not I found him wandering through the forest tonight. I figured I should bring him here instead of letting him rot outside."

"Nice to meet you, Jimmy," the man said as he held out his hand. "My name is Ralph and I've been coming here for years. You know, it's not often we get guests from that side, especially on a night like this. You couldn't have picked a better night to join us."

Ralph let out a shriek and nearly knocked me off balance as he skipped toward the largest group on the dance floor. Then he grabbed hold of a woman who was far taller than he was and swung her in a wide circle.

"What did he mean when he said . . ."

I didn't get to finish my question when Richard brought another man, slightly younger and much thinner than Ralph, and introduced us.

"Jimmy, I want you to meet Martin. He's one of my

closest friends here . . . used to be a doctor but . . . you could say he's retired."

"It's nice to meet you, Jimmy," the man said as he shook my hand. "Richard was just telling me how you two met. You were lost . . . is that it?"

"Yes, I was trying to find my way back to my car and it got too late. I was just happy he found me."

"Well, nothing happens by accident, my boy, especially here. You've stumbled across one of the most interesting places in the world, if you ask me. Like I said, nothing happens by accident, so you're here for a good reason. Good luck finding out what it is."

"Thank you," I said to him, growing more and more perplexed.

"Jimmy," Richard said, "why don't you walk around and meet people. Everyone here's real friendly, so you won't have any trouble getting into a conversation. I'll be over here chatting with Martin if you need me. Just have a fun time . . . and do some dancing, too."

"Okay," I said, wishing he wouldn't leave me alone. "I'll see who I meet and find you later."

I nervously began walking along the wall, saying hello to people as I passed. He was definitely right about how nice everyone was. Was it because I was the only new face in the crowd, or was this just how they were? I was also surprised that there was such a wide range of people living in this secluded little area in the middle of nowhere. They must have come from the whole region, and the fact that there were no cars or roads made the mystery even more perplexing. Perhaps that was what Ralph meant by his comment, about coming from the other side. But was he referring to me or to everyone there in the barn? I decided that it was simply a term they used for outsiders who stumbled into the area, either on purpose or by accident.

I was in the corner of the barn near a group of young girls, none of whom seemed to be over twelve. As far as I could tell, they were the only children at the dance, and I was also surprised that I didn't see any boys. It was one of the strangest and most interesting gatherings I had ever seen, but there was no way for me to know just how interesting it would soon become.

I stood in the corner and looked around at the different people I saw, all of whom seemed to be having a grand time. My eyes scanned the crowd trying to gather more information that might help me gain greater insight or maybe even figure out where I was. It was a cross section of so many races, sizes, and types; and best of all, none of the differences seemed to matter. The small groups seemed to shift and merge then shift again, giving the impression that everyone was equal, and that no one was the leader.

That's when I saw her. There was no way for me to be sure, but the sight of the woman standing against the far wall nearly took my breath away. I started to walk, but the shock I felt made it impossible for me to be aware of anyone or anything else around me. The closer I got, the more sure I was, but the impossibility of what I seemed to be looking at confused and mystified me. My eyes had to be playing tricks in the light, but I knew that it wasn't an illusion. I was only twenty feet away and I froze in place, feeling like I was about to faint.

It was Linda.

CHAPTER NINE

She ran forward to prevent me from collapsing on the floor.

"Are you okay?" she asked as she reached out and took hold of my arm. "You turned white and should probably sit down. Come over here with me."

She led me to an area where four or five hay bales rested against the wall, then guided me by the arm till I was sitting down. I placed my head between my legs to let the blood return to my brain and to shelter myself from the strange hallucination. My eyes were closed so I couldn't see my surroundings, but the fact remained that a woman who looked and sounded exactly like Linda was sitting next to me. And yet, it wasn't the woman I knew in middle age who had died when she was forty-three. The woman who sat next to me was in her early twenties, the same age Linda was when we met. Her hair was long and straight and she wore an outfit that I remembered well, a Laura Ashley dress that resembled a hipper version of something from *Little House in the Prairie*. I finally gained the courage to sit upright, then opened my eyes to look at her again. Her smile was bright, and her eyes possessed a brilliance that seemed otherworldly.

"My name is Linda," she said as she reached out her hand. I didn't know if I should offer mine in return or not, but finally did when I realized she wasn't going to pull away. "I saw you walking toward me, then you had this terrible pain in your face and I thought you were going to pass out."

"You said your name is Linda?" I asked without looking at her.

"Yes, that's what I said."

"Linda what? What's your last name?"

It was as if the question puzzled her. She looked toward the far wall of the barn as if she was thinking, then turned back to me and said: "I honestly don't know. It feels like I do, or that I should, but for the life of me I don't know what it is. I guess it isn't important."

"Do you know who I am?" I asked, finally getting up enough courage to look directly into her eyes. "You have to recognize me . . . do you know my name?"

She looked into my eyes and at my face. "Well, you do look very familiar, but I can't say I know who you are. Am I supposed to?"

It was as if something broke inside me and I wasn't able to hold myself together any longer. There was no question that this was the young woman I'd met in 1984, married, and raised a daughter with. She was also the woman who had been brutally murdered three and a half years earlier. That was the thing that disturbed me the most, the fact that the woman I had been grieving for was now sitting in front of me as if nothing had ever changed.

"Yes, you are supposed to," I said as I stood up from the hay bale. "It's me . . . your husband, or ex-husband, or whatever. Why don't you recognize me? And where the hell are we where this kind of thing feels so natural and normal?"

I looked over to the opposite side of the room and saw Richard staring straight at us. His look was both calming and urgent, as if he was willing me to keep calm and move forward. I turned back to Linda.

"I can guarantee we're not in hell," she said with a smile. "I wish I could help you more, but I honestly don't remember. All I know is that I came to this wonderful dance and you're here with me. You're a little confused, but you seem like a nice person so I want to help you. Can you tell me what I should do now?"

Her words were so innocent, like a child wanting to please a loved one or a lover opening her heart to a person she tenderly cares for. I decided to relax as best I could, and sat back down, then took a deep breath.

"I don't know what's happening here," I said, "but this is the most incredible and bizarre thing I've ever experienced, or even heard of." I took another deep breath, as if I knew the next step wouldn't be an easy one. "Let me try to explain why I'm so totally surprised. My name is Jimmy and you're Linda, the woman I married twenty-four years ago. The only thing is, you don't look like you did the last time I saw you. You were forty-three then, and now it looks like you're . . . ."

"Twenty-two . . . I'm not ashamed to tell you."

"Twenty-two? That's how old we both were when we met. We got married when we were twenty-three and then had a daughter. Her name is Angela. And then three and a half years ago something really bad happened." I stopped, willing myself to go on but not knowing if I should. I clenched my fists and let the words finally release. "You were killed . . . murdered. Last week a man confessed, and I became totally obsessed with this road, the one we almost died on when we were driving west after your funeral. I came back because I felt like I'd left a piece of myself behind and I had to find it before I'd be happy again. Then I meet this guy and he brings me here . . . to a barn dance. And who do I see on the other side of the room when I come to this barn dance? Well, only my former wife who was killed, as I said before. That's why I almost passed out when I saw you, and that's why I'm feeling pretty freaked out talking to you."

Linda started to laugh when I finished. "Wow, that's amazing . . . and that was me? It's incredible that I don't remember any of it."

"How can you not remember?" I said. "There's no question who you are. I'd know you anywhere. But why did you forget?"

The strangeness of my question struck me with dizzying effect. The idea that I would someday be face-to-face with Linda except in a dream had never occurred to me as a possibility. Was that what was happening . . . I was dreaming? I looked around at the other people who were dancing and standing around listening to the band and realized that as strange as it all was, it was very real. Dreams tend to be inconsistent, appearing one way this moment and another way the next. Except for the bizarre circumstances I encountered in the barn, nothing seemed out of place, with the exception of the fact that my wife, who had been dead for over three years, was sitting in front of me just as she had a thousand times before.

"That's just how it works," she said. "When you're here, none of that matters anymore. Only *now* matters, and right now I'm sitting having the most interesting conversation with you. I'm really enjoying this."

"You said *when you're here*. What does that mean? Where are we?"

"We're here, at the barn dance," she said as if it was completely obvious.

"I know that, but where is this barn dance? Where are we exactly?"

"I'm still not sure if I understand the question. I came to this dance because some friends told me it was really amazing and I should check it out. I have the feeling that I'm here because I was supposed to meet you, especially if I was your wife."

"So you know that you're dead, is that it?" The question seemed to startle her, and I immediately wished I hadn't asked it.

"Dead? What do you mean? None of us is dead."

"I'm sorry," I said. "I just thought that you realized . . ."

"No, you didn't understand . . . no one is dead anywhere. There's no real thing called *dead*. You may not realize that till you get here, but it's the truth. Nothing ever really dies."

"Then I'm really confused," I said, sitting back down next to her.

"And that's fine . . . just be confused then. There's nothing wrong with that. There are so many things that at first appear to be confusing, but then when everything settles you see that it's quite simple. I promise that this is like that. It may seem weird or strange now, but you'll see . . . it really isn't."

"Honey . . ." The words came out of my mouth so naturally, as if nothing had ever changed between us. "I don't know what's happening . . . all I know is that you're here with me, and that's amazing and scary at the same time. I've wanted this so much . . . to see you again. You have no idea what it was like to lose you like we did, so suddenly and violently. Then I hear that someone finally confessed and it was like tearing the wound open again. I had no idea that I would ever end up here, actually talking to you. I just don't understand what's happening, but I really like it."

"I don't know what's happening either," she said, "but I'm really happy to meet you, or to see you again, whichever is the case. You said that we were married before? Were we happy?"

"I wish I could say yes, but it ended very early. We got married when we were so young, and it was really my fault that it didn't work out. I thought I needed to make an impact on the world, and you just wanted to raise a family. If we had been a bit older and more mature, we might have been able to find a way, but we didn't. We always were best friends, though, and that really confused me because I never stopped being in love with you. I was trying to get you back till the day you died. It actually looked like it might happen because you were thinking about moving to Oregon to be with Angela and me. I thought that it really might be the moment I was waiting for."

"Can you show me?"

The question caught me off guard and I wasn't sure

how to respond. "Show you . . . how can I do that?" I finally asked.

"You can help me see what happened . . ." she said, ". . . how we lived . . . through your eyes. We've been given a great gift, and I don't want it to pass us by without getting the most out of it we can. I want to see what you're talking about because I have no memory of it. I can do that if you let me see through your eyes."

"Once again, how can I do that?" I asked, feeling my body tensing up. "You speak about it as if it's so natural and easy. I may not know where we are or what's happening, but what you're suggesting sounds impossible."

"The fact that you're here at all should tell you that nothing's impossible," she said. "All you have to do is relax and look into my eyes. I can do the rest."

"I don't have to do anything but look into your eyes?" I asked. "What happens then?"

"Then I follow you to a memory . . . that's all. That way I'll be able to see what you saw . . . we'll see it together. Do you think you can do that?"

I took a deep breath and relaxed back into the block of hay. "I'm not sure, but I'm willing to try. This has been the strangest experience of my life, so why stop now."

"Exactly . . . why stop now? Are you ready?"

"I am," I said, letting my eyes settle on hers. At first nothing seemed unusual or strange, except for the obvious. I could feel emotions begin to surface that were both comforting and disturbing, feelings of love and loss, calm and profound distress. I let them rush through my consciousness and had the thought that I shouldn't engage them in any way, just let them be present and take me where they chose. Then I had the sensation that I was moving forward, and it was only when I braced myself against the hay that I realized my position hadn't changed. Linda's eyes were growing larger in my vision, as if I was being pulled into her. Suddenly I had the sensation that they were no longer her eyes at all, but my own, and that my eyes were hers. As quickly as this thought arose, everything faded into a white mist, as if we were flying through a cloud with the sound of rushing wind filling my ears. A single consciousness emerged from inside the cloud, and I began to feel as if I was falling from the sky at a terrifying rate. I tried to slow the descent, but I didn't seem to have any control over what was happening. Then I heard a loud noise, almost like a large stick being broken against a tree.

I opened my eyes and realized that everything had changed.

CHAPTER TEN

I felt myself beginning to level off and realized I had arrived. My awareness seemed to be floating over an apartment building across the street from Loyola University on the north side of Chicago. I looked down the sidewalk and saw a much younger version of myself walking with someone I hadn't seen in over twenty years—Curtis, the friend who had introduced me to Linda. It was about a month after I'd graduated from Loyola, and Curtis had moved to Chicago from Minneapolis around the same time. My consciousness seemed to be poised above the entrance of a building, and I saw the two of us turn toward the entrance then push an intercom buzzer next to the front door. It was only then that I realized where we were—the building where I'd first met Linda and where we'd lived during the first year of our relationship. I tried to listen to the conversation the younger version of myself was having with Curtis, but the sound of the traffic made it too difficult to make out the words. Then I heard a muffled voice over the intercom.

"Who is it?" the voice asked. I recognized Colleen's voice. She was Linda's sister, who also lived in the building.

I remembered that Curtis had been in a short-lived relationship with her when he had first moved to the city, and it was that connection that ultimately led me to Linda.

"It's me," Curtis said as he leaned toward the speaker. "I'm with the friend I was telling you about."

"Okay," she said. "Come on in."

The buzzer sounded and we entered the building. I was hovering just above Curtis and my younger self as they walked down the hallway, then into a small elevator. My presence didn't seem to overfill the cramped space that would have been uncomfortable with three people, and it was only then that I heard the conversation.

"What time does her sister get back?" I asked him.

"If I were you I would forget about her," Curtis said to me. "I can't even count how many boyfriends she has. Every time I see her she's with someone new."

"I don't know," I said to him, "I have a good feeling about it. I'm also fine if nothing comes from it at all. I'm just excited to meet someone. I feel like I haven't been out of the woods since I left Loyola."

"Why did you take that job?" he asked. "You're out in the middle of nowhere giving retreats to a bunch of kids who don't even want to be there. You should come back to the city and have some fun with me."

"That's what I'm doing tonight. I just hope it turns out."

The elevator door opened and they stepped into the hallway. My spirit floated behind them as they walked to a door at the far end of the hallway and knocked. Seconds later a young woman with mid-length light brown hair stood in the doorway and gave Curtis a kiss.

"This is Jimmy," he said as he stepped to the side. "Tell

him not to get too excited about your sister."

"What has he been telling you?" Colleen asked as she leaned in to give me a hug. I liked her immediately. "Don't believe anything he says. My sister is wonderful. She's just a little picky, that's all. And why shouldn't she be? She's gorgeous."

We stepped into the room, and Colleen walked into the kitchen to stir a pot of soup she had on the stove.

"All I said was that he would have to stand in line if he wanted to have a chance," Curtis said.

"I'm not trying to have a chance with anyone," I said, uncomfortable with the whole conversation. "I'm just here to meet new people and have some fun. I'm not trying to pick up . . ."

"Listen," Colleen said, holding the wooden spoon in the air to make her point. "I would love for my sister to meet someone other than the guys she's been hanging out with. She's too good for them, and from everything Curtis told me about you . . . well, I'm excited for her to meet you, that's all."

A half hour passed and they, or rather we, were sitting in the living room eating the soup Colleen had prepared. I was impressed by her open enthusiasm and playful manner, and as I hovered above the scene watching it unfold, I was amazed by how many of the details I had forgotten over the years. We usually don't recognize the pivotal moments that shape our lives until much later, long after most of the features fade from our minds. In a short while Linda would walk through the door, and I knew exactly what I would feel. My pulse would begin to race and my entire body would feel as if it were vibrating. Though I wouldn't know it at the time, she'd had a similar reaction, though it took years for her to admit that to me. It was a strange experience to watch one aspect of me completely oblivious to what was about to occur, while another, the older me, hovered above the scene, all too aware.

There was a knock on the door and Colleen stood up. "That must be her," she said. "She lives downstairs, and this is the time she always gets home."

I could feel both aspects of myself, the one sitting on the couch and the one hovering above the scene, turn to face her as she entered. It was only at that moment that I understood what Linda had said to me at the barn before I was pulled into her eyes and into this scene. She said that she would watch everything that happened *through* me, as if she would be seeing everything through the lens of my consciousness. I could suddenly feel her presence, as if the Linda on the other side of the door and the one watching the scene with me were energetically connected. Though I was experiencing a scene that had occurred twenty-five years earlier, the bridge that connected the past and the present was unbearably thin, and I could feel it shaking beneath my feet.

When Colleen opened the door, it was as if time stopped. Linda looked exactly as she had when I had seen her in the barn moments earlier, though it had been many years since I'd actually met her walking into her sister's apartment. If time really is an illusion, then I was experiencing its onslaught firsthand, and the effect was one of deliberate and profound confusion. At first she didn't look at me, but stepped through the door as someone foreign and unattached, interacting as if she really didn't belong there. I turned to watch my counterpart's reaction, the younger Jimmy, and though he desperately tried to hide the sudden energy he felt, it seeped through the cracks of his being in a way that seemed so obvious. He, or I, stood up from the couch but resisted the urge to step toward her. To my younger self it was all still a mystery, and though he felt the unexpected rush of light and grace, there was no way for him to know if it was more than his imagination. I, of course, knew that it was so much more.

Curtis walked toward Linda and gave her a hug, then turned toward me and said: "I brought a friend with me who's visiting for a few days. Jimmy's the reason I came to Chicago. We went to high school together in Minnesota and he talked me into moving south. Jimmy, this is Colleen's sister, Linda." I watched the setup with appreciation and amusement. Because I had the luxury of knowing details that were still hidden from everyone else in the room, I knew that Linda already knew I would be there, and that she had no intention of giving me any reasonable consideration, at least not outwardly. Just as Curtis had said, she was a single, beautiful young woman who drew the attention of many men, and the last thing she wanted was to add one more to the list. She finally turned to face me, and I watched for a spark of recognition or empathy. Instead, all I felt was a steely resolve, and even the aspect of me floating near the ceiling wondered how I would overcome it.

"It's nice to meet you," she said politely as she reached out her hand. Then she turned back to Colleen. "What's happening tonight? I have a class I have to go to in the morning, so I can't stay out too late."

"I don't think we have anything planned yet," Colleen said. "They just got here a little while ago, and we really haven't talked about it."

"I heard about a hypnotist over at Sally's Stage on Western Avenue who's apparently really entertaining," Curtis offered. "If we want we could go there for a while and check it out, then maybe over to Cheers for a couple of drinks."

Cheers was a sports bar only a few doors down from the building where Linda and Colleen lived, and had been a favorite of mine while attending Loyola. With only a slight resemblance to the bar on the popular television series, it maintained just enough neighborhood attitude to make it feel both comfortable and interesting. Curtis's plan was soon adopted, and a half hour later we were on our way to Sally's Stage to see the hypnotist.

"Tell me more about yourself," Linda said hours later as we sat down at a corner table at Cheers. The hypnotist had proven to be great entertainment, and it was time to settle in for end-of-the-evening drinks. I was happy and surprised that she was finally showing interest in me, since she seemed to spend the entire evening huddled close to her sister avoiding contact. Colleen and Curtis had disappeared outside, which left the two of us alone.

"Well, I graduated from Loyola about a month ago," I began, "and I took a job working at a little retreat center west of the city. It's pretty far away, and I don't have my own car, so it makes it hard to come back to the old neighborhood."

"A retreat center?" she asked. "What kind of retreats do you do?"

"Catholic high schools send their kids there. Let's just say that they're not too willing when they come, but usually by the end they've opened up and have a good time. I really love it, to tell you the truth. I had no idea what I wanted to do when I got out of school, and this seems to fit my personality."

"I just got back from a retreat myself," she said, smiling in a way that told me I had finally sparked her interest. "There's a book called *The Handbook to Higher Consciousness* that I study, and I went to a workshop last weekend to learn more."

"Tell me more about the book," I said, trying to keep the conversation moving.

"This guy named Ken Keyes wrote it. He became a quadriplegic from polio when he was a kid, and he developed a process called *The Science of Happiness*, which is pretty amazing when you think about it."

"Why is that amazing?"

"This is someone who could very easily feel like a victim, but he doesn't. He doesn't believe that happiness is something that happens to us randomly, but through letting go of our separating beliefs and addictions. There are all sorts of tools and techniques he teaches. That's pretty much what we did all weekend."

As I watched the scene from above, I could feel Linda from the barn trying to remember. It was as if we were joined together in such a way that I could feel her emotions and she could feel mine. She was touched by the love I was feeling as I watched the scene, and I could feel her wishing she could recall more, like an amnesiac longing to repossess the memories that shaped her life. I, on the other hand, felt like I was watching my favorite film in the world, the scene when I met the love of my life, and I didn't want it to end.

"We did a bit of dream therapy at the retreat as well," she continued.

"This may sound ignorant, but what in the world is dream therapy?"

She laughed and reached across the table to touch my arm. The feeling invigorated me.

"You really need to get with the times," she said. "It's a whole new world out there, especially with all the New Age philosophy and techniques and things. Dream therapy means you watch and remember your dreams, then interpret them. Everything in your dream is a symbol, and if you learn what the symbols mean then you can use them to understand what's going on in your life. Sometimes the things we think about right before we go to sleep can influence what we dream as well."

"I don't even want to tell you what I think about before I go to sleep," I said nervously.

"Now you have to tell me."

"Well, you know how we make up little tricks or games that help us fall asleep?" I said, wondering if I was about to make a mistake. "I have one that I do almost every night, but I'll tell you right now, it's kind of weird."

"Go on."

"I imagine that I have this superpower that I can't tell anyone about. It's like I have the ability to make people feel certain illnesses just by focusing my mind on them, and not just one person, but I can also make huge numbers of very specific people feel things, too."

"This sounds sick," she said as she leaned forward, clearly engaged. "You actually think about this before you go to sleep?"

"Yes . . . and I can't believe I'm telling you about it. Anyway, I even imagine that I can cause people to die if I want, but only if they really deserve it. For example, if I want I can focus my energy on every single person who ever murdered a child and make them feel terribly sick or even die. It's a power that could come in handy, if you think about it. Imagine being able to convince every terrorist in the world that if they don't give up their hatred and terrorist plots, then they'll all die at exactly 2 PM on Tuesday. I would find some way of having it published in every newspaper in the world so they would have fair warning, then when the time comes, everyone who doesn't repent dies. Imagine how quickly we could clean up the world with that kind of skill."

"I can't believe you've thought this through so completely," she said. "You're really sick."

"Not really. It's just a weird little thing I do that helps me sleep. It does make me wonder what would happen if any of us had that superpower, though."

"What do you mean?"

"I think I'm just going to stop there," I said, forcing myself to quit. "This wasn't something I thought I would ever tell anyone, especially in a situation like this."

"I'm not sure what you mean when you say *a situation like this*."

As the older me watched myself sitting there at the table, I realized that "his" stomach was spinning like a tornado. Had I said too much, revealing more of my heart than I intended? There was little doubt about what I was feeling—ever since I saw her walk in the door of her sister's apartment I had felt lovestruck, and there was nothing I could do about it. At the same time I was also smart enough to read the signs, and every one said she wasn't that interested. My only recourse was to win her over in due time, assuming, of course, that I was capable of taking my time, something that's usually against my natural rhythm and inclination. I wanted to rush into the fray and announce my objective with vigor, securing her affection as soon as humanly possible. I was already kicking myself for telling her about the ridiculous ritual I had developed to fall asleep. If there was any hope at all, it had likely been squandered by then. But to my surprise, Linda's open smile seemed to indicate that I was closer to my goal than I originally guessed. She neither backed away nor energetically recoiled when I decided to be honest about my feelings.

"Well, I don't know . . ." I said, pressing forward with caution. "I guess I mean that we're here having such a great time talking, and I really wish that Colleen and Curtis would just stay outside."

It must have been the right thing to say since she laughed and pushed herself back from the table. "They left a long time ago," she said. "They went back to her place, which means you're on your own."

"Oh," I said, shocked by the fact that I hadn't realized what was happening. "Then I guess I'm lucky you're still here. You could have ditched me a long time ago if you wanted."

"I don't think that will happen," she said, and for the first time I felt her relax and consider the possibility that there really was something happening between us.

"You don't?" I said, still careful not to move too fast. "Then I would say that's very good news."

We sat looking into each other's eyes without saying a word, and I could feel the intensity moving up toward the ceiling where I was still hovering. Linda reached out and took my hand, and it created what felt like a spark that jolted through the older me and began pulling my spirit down toward the table. An instant later I was at eye level, facing her with a closer perspective than my even younger self, and I felt myself being pulled into her eyes just as I had been before. They seemed to envelop my entire being, and I felt the familiar sensation of being pulled out of the world where they lived into the other that I still wasn't sure really existed at all. Seconds later I opened my eyes and realized I was back in the barn, with Linda sitting across from me.

CHAPTER ELEVEN

I took a deep breath.

"You really loved me, didn't you?" she asked when she saw what it took for me to recover from the vision.

"Yes," I said, still slightly shaky. "I always loved you. No matter what happened between us, that didn't change."

"And that was where it all began," she continued. "Thank you for helping me see that. It must have been such a beautiful night."

"So you don't have any memory of it at all, and you were able to see the whole thing through my eyes?"

"No, I don't remember anything, and yes, I did see it all through you. I don't know if that makes sense or not . . ."

"It doesn't, and yet it does," I said. "It did feel like we were watching it together, though at the same time I didn't feel you at all. I don't think I can explain it in any other way."

"What happened after that?"

"Well, I remember walking you back to your apartment and kissing you on the doorstep. I'll never forget that kiss. We dated for a while after that and got married about a year later."

"Tell me more about our daughter," she said. "What's she like?"

"She's so much like both of us," I told her, suddenly finding myself comfortable with the conversation. "She has your beauty and my ingenuity, I guess. People often say that she looks like the perfect mix between the two of us, though I think she looks more like you." I paused and took a long look at the woman sitting next to me. "I remember how beautiful you were, especially when we first met, just like you are now. You were and continue to be the most beautiful woman I've ever seen."

"You're just seeing me like this now because it's how you best remember me," she said.

"What do you mean? This isn't how you usually look?"

"There is no particular *look* or *way of looking* here. You're seeing me in the way I once was, but now none of that matters. You could see me as a child, or when I was forty-three. I'm not limited to any of that, just as you're not limited to the way you look right now."

She smiled at me as if there was something deeper to what she said than what was obvious. I thought for a moment, then dismissed it as my imagination.

"So once again . . . where are we?" I asked. "I know we're at a barn dance and everything, but obviously something bigger is happening. Can you tell me where all this actually is?"

Linda stood up without answering and took me by the hand, then led me to a table where an elderly woman was serving glasses of white wine from a cardboard table. She smiled as we approached.

"Look at the two of you," the woman said as she handed us two crystal goblets that seemed out of place at a barn dance. "You look so beautiful together."

"We're apparently married," Linda said. "I didn't even know."

"Well, that's a wonderful thing to discover, being married and all. You have a wonderful time at the dance."

"I'm sorry," Linda remembered as we walked away. "What did you ask again?"

"I asked where we are. It seems like you keep avoiding the question. I met a man down by the creek when I was lost, and he told me about the barn. Now I see that it's more than just an ordinary dance, and I need to know where this is."

"Let me see if I can put this in a way you'll understand," she said as she stopped and looked at me. "We're somewhere between Heaven and Earth . . . I thought you knew that already."

"Somewhere in between?" I asked. "But how is that possible?"

"It's the truth," she said, "but in a way it isn't the truth at all, because it makes it seem as if Heaven and Earth are two different places. They really aren't, but that would be a whole different conversation."

We started walking again in the direction where Richard was standing. He smiled as we approached as if he knew exactly what was happening.

"It's nice to see you made a friend," he said to me. Then he turned to Linda. "I don't think we've met. My name is Richard."

"I'm Linda. It's my first time here. I heard about you, though. I have a friend named Susan on the other side and she's been here before and met you."

"Of course, I know Susan well. I don't see her here tonight."

"She told me that it was important that I come," Linda continued as she looked over at me. "I think I know why now. I guess I was supposed to meet this guy . . . though I'm not sure if *meet* is the right word since we've definitely met before."

"Yes, you have," Richard said as he looked straight at me, giving the impression that he knew this meeting would occur. "I found him wandering around not too far from here and had a strong feeling he was meant to come. I wasn't sure why . . . but now I know."

"How often does this happen?" Linda asked, referring to the barn dance as far as I could tell. "It's really nice and I'd love to tell others about it."

"It happens every night," Richard told her. "It's a special place, and special places sometimes have a life of their own. I'm also not sure if you're supposed to mention it to too many others. We don't want it to get too crowded."

"You two seem to be having a conversation I can't join," I said. "Two hours ago I was lost in the forest and now I'm at a dance with my wife who died three and a half years ago. Don't get me wrong, I'm overjoyed to be here and don't want to ever leave, but the whole thing has me feeling a bit off balance."

"Trust me," Linda said, "I'm just as off balance as you are. If you saw where I just came from you'd understand."

Richard looked at me and smiled. "And with that I'm going to let the two of you have your time together. I'll be around if you need me."

Richard gave me a pat on the back, smiled, then walked away, joining in on a conversation between three men who were examining an ancient-looking tractor in the corner of the barn.

"What do you want to do?" Linda asked as if we were free to go anywhere we wanted.

I thought for a moment and said: "Why don't we go for a walk. There's a beautiful stream a little way in that direction . . ."

"I can't do that," she said. "This is as far as we can go together . . . the barn. Whatever we decide, it has to be here."

"Really? You can't leave the barn?"

"I can leave . . . but not with you. If I leave, we won't be together anymore, at least not like this. So if we want to keep talking, we need to do it here."

"I'd like to be able to understand what that means," I said to her.

"Maybe later," she said as she led me back to the bales of hay where we began our conversation. "For now I want to hear more about what happened. I know it doesn't matter, but I'm still curious about it. I can't remember anything really, except for an occasional flash that doesn't make much sense."

We sat down and she faced me. I wondered if it would be okay for me to tell her the details and how she might react. I also didn't want to relive it myself, especially in this situation with her sitting so close.

"To tell you the truth, we really don't know what happened," I said. "There were no witnesses, nothing was stolen, and it took over three years to find someone who claimed responsibility. I spoke with you on the phone that night, and everything was fine. I told you about Angela and you cried."

"Why did I cry?" she asked.

"You cried because you realized how much Angela loved you. You used to wonder about that because she wasn't exactly the sweetest daughter when she was a teenager. But then she grew up and the two of you started to have a real relationship . . . a friendship. I was so happy that you had the chance to really get to know and like each other, even if it was so short. I know that she misses it so much and feels like she lost something so important to her."

"I promise you we'll see each other again," Linda said in a serious voice. "There's one thing we always take with us from one world to the next, and that's the love we share. It never leaves us, and is like a bridge that always brings us back together. Will you tell her that? I want her to know that the love we shared was more important than anything else."

I could feel the emotions beginning to rise within me again. "Yes, I will tell her."

"And also let her know that everything's going to turn out for her. I have a strong feeling that she's going to turn into an amazing woman."

"You're right about that," I said to her. "You wouldn't believe how she's been turning her life around, even though it was a big setback when she heard that someone finally confessed to killing you. That was a blow for all of us, even though it was good to hear that there was some progress. I wish there was more you could tell us about what happened that night."

"You need to remember that I don't know anything about what happened," she said with eyes so open and clear that my argument almost faded away on its own. "On this side of the veil none of those things matter, and that's why

I'm not holding on to any of it. The only thing I know is that in the end we're all innocent, especially in the eyes of God, and that's one of the hardest things for people to understand. Some people want to believe in a God that condemns and punishes us for our mistakes, but in reality God looks past all of them and sees us for who we really are, not who we're pretending to be."

"You talk as if you know the guy."

"Guy? What if I told you God's a Mexican woman with the biggest and warmest hug in the universe? You'd be surprised, trust me."

"This is something I didn't even consider before," I said to her. "You can tell me things about Heaven that no one else knows about, and about God. What's it like, and how do you live when you're on the other side?"

"All I'll tell you is this," she said as she leaned closer to me. "It's like nothing you'd imagine and everything you could hope for. Beyond that, words won't work. They can't even come close."

"But you said that we're in kind of an in-between place right now. What's to stop me from following you and going to Heaven before my time?"

"The point I'm trying to make is that you're always in Heaven," she said. "Heaven is all around us all the time. The question is—are we willing to open our eyes and see it?"

She paused and looked at me, as if she was expecting an answer. Everything she said was starting to make sense, but I was afraid to step out on my own, as if it was easier than taking a risk.

"Why are you stopping?" I asked her. "I really don't know how to answer."

"You do know, you're just afraid to say it. And I understand why . . . in fact, it's a big part of the reason you're here. You're here because it's easier for you to hold on to the sorrow you feel than let yourself fully heal . . . to move on. It's easier for you to be in grief than to realize that everything happens for a reason, and that I actually chose the way I died. And because you can't look at those things, it's easier to hold on to your anger as well. You said before that everything was stirred up again because someone finally confessed to my murder. Then you became obsessed with the road where you, Angela, and Heather almost died. You had to get back there because there were answers for you, even if they were at the bottom of that cliff."

"So it's true . . . that really was my car at the bottom of the cliff?"

"There are a few places on this earth where the lines that usually keep the different worlds separate begin to blur, and they actually come into contact with one another. This is one of those places. Usually these lines are very distinct and the two never intersect, but every now and then we find a place where possibilities become the tools that help us learn, and that's what happened to you. There was one timeline where you slid another five inches and the car went over the edge. You all died that night, and all three of you are here in Heaven learning new and really amazing lessons. But there was another aspect of you, the part you chose to be consciously aware of, that stopped just in time. You came to the edge but didn't go over, and went on to continue life on the physical plane. There's a reason that happened and that's what you need to learn . . . why you're still here and not in that car."

"I'm here because I want to be with you," I said. "You

have no idea how hard this has been for me, knowing that we would never be together again and having to deal with the terrible way you died. I don't want to leave. If this is Heaven, then why can't I just stay and be with you here forever?"

"Because you're not ready," she explained. Her smile seemed to widen for a second, as if she was touched by the thought, then returned to the wizened sage-like face that now seemed so natural to her. "You didn't die like I did, so it's not time for you to stay here. There's still work for you to do, but you'll only be able to finish it if you learn the lesson you came here to learn."

"So I'm definitely still alive?" I asked her.

"Oh, I guarantee that you're very much alive, and so am I. It's easy to think that our bodies define what it means to be alive or dead. If you're breathing and walking around, then you must be alive, and if you're stiff and the blood stops pumping through your veins, then you must be dead. Right? But what if that isn't how it works at all? You're here with me right now, and as far as you can tell, I'm alive. You seem alive to me as well. What I'm saying is that being alive is not something that depends on your body, but your soul."

"You keep telling me that there's something I need to learn before I can leave. That makes it easy for me, then. I just won't learn anything, then I can stay here."

Linda laughed in a way that was so familiar to me. Her head fell back, and the sound that boomed from her was so distinct and unexpected. "I can see this isn't going to be easy," she said. "I wish it was that simple because I would love for you to stay. You're so funny, but you can't trick your way into Heaven like that. And it doesn't matter how funny you are, even though it would be a really nice change. So many people here are too serious. It's not that they're morbid or anything, but Heaven is supposed to be a joyous place, and most people I know don't laugh enough."

"Then I could be of some help. I can stay and lighten the mood."

"That would be wonderful, but no. You really do need to learn whatever lesson you came to learn, then go back to Angela. She needs you there."

"Can you tell me what lesson I need to learn?"

"I wish I could, but you have to discover it on your own. All I'll tell you is that the lesson you need to learn is the same lesson for all of us. The details and the reasons may change, but the lesson is ultimately the same."

It was only then that I noticed the band had stopped playing, the lights were being turned off, and most of the people were beginning to leave through a door to the rear of the barn. There was a bright light coming through the door, as if someone had the headlights of a large truck pointed straight in. Linda turned around and looked at this, then turned back to me.

"I have to leave now, but I really enjoyed talking to you."

I felt my heart suddenly speed up as if I had just run a four-minute mile. "Linda, wait, you can't just leave. I don't want to go without you."

"I don't mean I'm leaving for good," she said, smiling. "I just have to leave for now. We can only stay here for a while, then we have to return."

"Why can't I go with you?" I asked, hoping she would change her mind.

"You can't go through that door yet," she said as she again looked at all the people who were passing through into the white light. "Someday, but not now. I'll find you again tomorrow. We still have so many things to talk about."

Linda turned around and started to walk toward the others. When she was halfway to the door, she turned back to me with an expression I hadn't noticed on her face before.

"How is she?" Linda asked me. "How is my daughter? I think I can remember her, which is really unusual. We usually aren't able to remember too many details from our lives, but I think I can still see her face." Then she paused and looked up toward the ceiling as if she was feeling something very profound. "I must have loved her very much."

Tears began to fall down my cheeks. "Yes, you did love her very much . . . and she loved you. You'd be very proud of our daughter."

"I am very proud of her, and I'm proud of you, too." Then she smiled. "I'll see you tomorrow, okay?"

"Okay . . . I'll see you tomorrow."

She turned toward the door and seconds later she passed through. The barn was suddenly dark, and I realized that Richard was standing a few feet behind me.

"Come on, Jimmy, we should probably go, too."

I turned and followed him out the opposite door, the one that led back to the world I no longer understood at all.

Chapter Twelve

Richard and I walked the path that ran alongside the stream with the full moon lighting our way. He suggested we not talk about what happened until we arrived back at his house, which was at least fifteen minutes away. I was in a daze, completely incapable of wrapping my mind around what had just occurred. For over an hour I had been involved in a conversation with the one woman I thought it was impossible to ever see again, and yet it felt completely natural. We had somehow found each other between Heaven and Earth, as if the barn was the one place in the world where dreams really do come true. But what would I do with this information and experience? There was no way I could call anyone since we were well outside cell-phone range. And even if I could, what would I say? Should I call Angela and tell her I just saw her mother and she hardly remembered her? I decided that the only thing I could do was wait and see what happened next. After all, there was still tomorrow.

I could see the dim lights inside Richard's house as we approached and caught the scent of burning wood well before we arrived. He walked in front of me and almost seemed to float slightly off the ground, though I was almost sure I was imagining this. But who was he, and what was the role he played in this amazing drama? His presence was strong and solid, and there was a profound patience that surrounded him and every word he spoke. His voice was like warm brandy that moved slowly over my consciousness and through my mind. I had met so many spiritual teachers and leaders throughout my life, and yet Richard, even in the short period of time I knew him, seemed to be a step above them all. He didn't need books or degrees to back up his pedigree. His heart seemed to be enough, as well as the wisdom that flowed from him so effortlessly.

"Come inside and relax," he said as he opened the front door. "I know you have many questions about what happened tonight, and I'll try to answer as many as I can. But for now it's important that we center ourselves and maybe even get something to eat."

"Why did you tell me not to say anything till we got here?" I asked him.

Richard was already walking toward the kitchen and spoke over this shoulder. "Because you never know who's listening," he said. I looked to see if he was joking, but judging from his serious tone and the look on his face I guessed he wasn't. "As you can already tell, this forest is very special. There are things that happen here that don't happen anywhere else." He reached above his head and pulled a bottle of wine from a rack in the corner. "I make this myself, which is why there's no label. It's kind of like this forest, unpredictable and mysterious. Hope you like it."

"Tell me more about the forest," I said as I sat down on a stool. "The man I met at the hotel told me this area was sacred, but I didn't think he meant this."

"I think that pretty well explains it," Richard said as he popped the cork. "There are only a few areas in the world where things like this happen. Imagine it like a crease in a piece of fabric . . . it makes it hard to tell where one world ends and another one begins, and yet it's still one fabric." He poured a bit of red wine into the glass and took a sip. "Not too bad . . . want some?"

"Yes, of course. So you're saying that this is one of those places where they come together. Is it the whole forest?"

"No, it's not," he said as he poured me a glass. "The whole area is important and mystical, but there's only one spot where the worlds blend together."

"At the barn."

"Yes, the barn," he said as he touched my glass to his own. "I built that barn about ten years ago when I first arrived. I needed to find a way to contain what was happening, or maybe give it some protection. Until then everything happened out in the open, and that's why the natives avoided the area. It was too hard for them to understand, and for many years only the holy men of the tribe were allowed to come. Of course that all changed, and one day I was hiking along the creek and I saw something I didn't understand. Before long I put it all together, and have been here ever since."

"So there's no town or village nearby where all those people live?" I asked, as if I needed reassurance.

"Not in the traditional sense, but it sure feels like it sometimes. The barn is a gathering place where people meet and get to feel like they used to feel. There are some who come nearly every night, and others who only come once. That was the first time I ever saw Linda, so she must have known . . ."

". . . that I would be there?"

"Yes, somehow it all came together as it was meant to," he continued. "You said that you became obsessed with this area because you almost died here. It was calling you back. Somehow you knew that this was going to happen."

"Which brings up another very important question," I said. "What about that BMW at the bottom of the cliff? Linda said that we made a choice in that moment, that in one timeline we didn't go over the edge, while in another we did. Does that make any sense to you?"

"Before I answer, you'll have to tell me about the BMW. You didn't tell me about that before."

I had forgotten that I'd decided not to mention the car in our first conversation. It only took a few minutes to explain since I didn't have any real answers at that point. All I knew for sure was that the car was very similar to my own, but then Linda seemed to indicate that it really was mine.

"So Linda explained the whole theory of multiple universes to you?" he asked. "It doesn't surprise me at all. It's not as if quantum science isn't finding out about this on its own. It may be a new idea to modern physicists, but to the mystics there's nothing new about it at all."

"Are you telling me that you believe it's my car?" I asked him. "But how was it possible for me to see it if it exists on another timeline or quantum field?"

"As you've already learned, normal laws don't seem to apply here," Richard said as he started rummaging through the cupboard for something to eat. "This is a very unusual area. It's not just the spot where the barn is built, but all around us. If that's what Linda said, then I would believe her." Then he stopped what he was doing and turned around. "I have to admit, though, that I've never seen a BMW at the bottom of the cliff."

"It was right at the spot where we almost went over three years ago. It was the same model, color, and year; and though I can't be absolutely sure, it definitely seemed like my car."

"As I said, I've never seen it. But that doesn't mean it isn't there."

"So you think that my obsession with the area was a way to get me to come back," I said. "But how is all that possible?"

"Jimmy, you're trying to comprehend something with your brain that can only be understood with your heart. Your brain is never going to understand this. As you said, it's impossible. But sometimes the things that seem impossible to the intellect are really quite simple. I wish I could tell you how it all works, but I can't. I've been here for ten years now, and have seen things that few people would believe. If I tried to figure it all out I would go crazy. Instead, I accept that this place is special, and it's giving me a glimpse of something that's usually only seen on the other side. What an honor to be a witness to all this! So few have shared it with me."

"So there have been others who came to the barn with you?" I asked.

"A few . . . people like you who found the place on their own and had something to learn. That's the one thing I can tell you that's been true for everyone . . . there was something they came to learn. When you figure out what that is for you, then your obsession will stop."

"Why would I want it to stop? I'm thinking about building a little house right next to yours and living here full time. Think about it . . . this is the only place in the world where I can still be with Linda. Why would I want to leave?"

"Nice try, but it doesn't work like that. You can't use the barn to avoid life, or to be with a person who is no longer part of your world. It's a gift, for sure, but not one you can control. If you try to abuse it, then there's no telling what might happen. I've only seen that once."

"What do you mean?" I asked. "Please tell me what happened."

"Well, about five years ago a woman came here because she had lost her son in a car crash. She lived in Ohio and about a year later just started driving west until she decided to leave I-80 like you did. When she got to this part of the highway, she left her car and just started walking through the forest without having any idea where she was going. I didn't find her for three days. She was starving and had nearly frozen to death, but she knew she had to be here. Of course I brought her to the barn because I never question when God sends someone. I just figure that it's beyond my limited comprehension.

"Anyway, she went to the dance and of course saw her son. It was really beautiful, just as it was when you saw Linda, but then everything changed. She only had the one meeting, but she refused to leave. Night after night she came to the party, and when her son didn't show up she made a terrible scene. I was afraid she was going to ruin it for everyone, but then a search party came along after they found her car and they took her away. As far as anyone was concerned, she was lost in the forest and had gone a bit crazy. She tried to tell them what happened, but they figured she had broken under the strain."

"Did they find you or the barn?"

"Luckily not," he said. "They were so close, but nothing like that happened."

"Linda promised me she would be back again tomorrow night." I said. "Is that unusual?"

"Nothing's unusual here. I've gotten used to accepting whatever happens. It's rare for people to find this place . . . I mean, maybe eleven or twelve over the ten years I've been around, but it's always important. I can honestly say that every person has left with some lesson. That's why I know that it will be the same for you."

"And I suppose you don't know what my lesson is?"

"Nope. And if I did, I wouldn't tell you. That's something you need to find for yourself, otherwise it won't integrate in the same way, and the fact that Linda asked you to stay means quite a bit. Of all the people who have been here before, only a few have had more than one meeting. That's quite a gift."

Richard had already started heating up a can of soup on the gas stove. I looked around and realized that there was no refrigerator, and aside from the stove, no ordinary household appliances at all.

"How do you get gas and electric?" I asked. "You're too far from civilization here, and I doubt they strung a line just for you."

"No, they didn't. I go into town now and then and get what I need. The batteries are replenished by solar, and the gas I just refill. I have everything I need, and actually get along just great."

"And I'm assuming you don't have any friends other than the ones from the barn. Isn't that a little strange?"

"I have to say that it isn't. It took a little getting used to at first, but after a while, it became so normal, no different from any other community of friends. Some of them come back nearly every night and give me all the interaction I need. Then there are the first-timers, like Linda. Sometimes they come to meet a specific person, like you, and other times they wander in and never leave. I think it gives them a nostalgic feeling to be there, but it's never the same."

"What do you mean?" I asked.

"You'll find out. I don't want to tell you everything or it'll ruin the surprise. You wouldn't want me to do that, would you?"

"I'm not sure how to answer that."

"Just trust me. I won't lead you astray, and no matter what happens tomorrow night, I'll be there for you. You can count on that."

* * *

I woke up the next morning with the sun in my eyes and darted out of bed to start the day. There was no confusion about where I was or why I was there, a usual experience for one who spends much of their time on the road. I knew that I was in the middle of a mountainous ravine where the laws of time and space no longer operated as they did in most places, and that somewhere not far away, there was a barn where people from Heaven were gathering to line-dance and drink fine chardonnay. It wasn't at all surprising that Linda would find her way into such an interesting crowd, but it was nice to see that her taste in wine had definitely improved. I often teased her about the box of blush she kept in the refrigerator that seemed to last up to a month before needing to be replaced. We brought her ashes to Oregon after the funeral and buried them at a small retreat center I own outside Ashland. Angela and a few friends who knew Linda joined us, and I bought the cheapest bottle of red zinfandel I could find and shared it with the group, then poured some onto the ground for her. She would have liked the joke.

I dressed and went to find Richard. It had been nearly nightfall when we'd met the previous day, and I wondered what someone like him did while the sun was still high. The entire situation, after all, was well outside my normal range of experience. Most of all, I wanted to know when we could go back to the barn. It seemed unlikely that the phenomenon was reserved strictly for nighttime use, though the party definitely appeared to be an evening affair. For all I knew there were also daytime events, or even a "Heavenly Happy Hour" with little snacks and half-off drinks. The thought made me laugh as I walked around the house realizing I was alone.

I stepped outside and called Richard's name. Seconds later he appeared carrying an armful of sticks destined for the fireplace.

"Give me a hand," he said. "There's a whole pile behind those trees over there. I'm starting to run low and went hunting for wood early this morning."

I filled my arms with as much of the kindling as I could handle, then followed him to the back of the house and placed it on the large pile. Next to a small shed I saw a large ax and chopping block, and the shed was filled with seasoned firewood. It was amazing how well equipped he was in such an isolated spot. I could see how easy it would be to stay there, especially considering that he had an endless supply of interesting company.

"I'll bet it never gets boring around here," I said to him.

"That's one way of putting it," he said as he wiped his brow with a white handkerchief then placed it back in his pocket. "For someone who lives in the woods without another living soul around, I sure have a lot of friends."

I caught the joke. Richard's friends were not living, at least not in the usual sense, and yet it seemed that his relationships with them were completely ordinary. Many returned to the barn every night and had for years. When Richard first arrived and decided to build a structure to contain the phenomenon, he enlisted their help. It was strange for me to think of these men who had lived long lives in the world hammering nails and carrying planks. Then I remembered my experience from the previous night and how real everyone seemed, especially Linda. When she held my hand it felt no different from when she had done the same as a living woman. Of course this thought led to others that were even more confusing. What about human interactions that were more intimate? I asked Richard about this the first chance I had.

"Well, it's actually a good question," he said as he poured me a cup of coffee. "I can't say that I've ever seen anything like that before, but then again, I don't think it's impossible. Why . . . you weren't thinking . . ."

"Of course not," I said, feeling the blood rushing to my face. "I would never think something like that . . . at least not right away or without . . ."

"I would put that thought out of your mind right away.

I said that you're here to learn something, not to rekindle an old romance."

"Forget I asked," I said, embarrassed. "This is all so new to me, and I just want to know what the parameters are."

"I doubt there are many parameters," he continued. "That's the nature of the spot, isn't it? It defies what should and should not be happening. I doubt there's more than one or two other places in the world where this happens. The system was originally designed to keep this world here and the other one wherever it belongs, but I guess the real lesson is that in the end they all coincide."

"They all collide in the place I just happened to have nearly died," I said. "I feel like I just won the lottery."

Chapter Thirteen

We started walking toward the barn as the last remnants of daylight streaked through the sky, but by the time we arrived, the entire forest was completely dark. I could hear music as we approached, and was surprised it wasn't bluegrass as it had been the previous evening. I couldn't be sure as we approached the door, but it sounded classical.

"I need to tell you something before we go inside," Richard said to me. "Don't expect anything to be the same. It rarely repeats itself."

"What do you mean?" I asked, but he was already opening the door and didn't answer.

I was first struck by the sound of food being served and light conversation underneath the music of the string quartet I saw in the corner of the room. As I stepped inside I was completely shocked—a fine restaurant had replaced the barn dance, four crystal chandeliers were hanging from the ceiling, and a marble staircase led to the upper dining hall. A bar at the far side of the large room was filled with men wearing fine tuxedos and smoking long cigars, laughing and talking in small groups. Then I looked over to the door through which Linda and the others had disappeared the night before and saw well-dressed couples and others walking through, as if from a line that snaked in from the other side. A maître d' escorted them two by two to their tables.

I looked around hoping to see Linda, but it didn't seem like she was there. I turned to Richard. "What's happening? What happened to the barn dance?"

"As I said, nothing stays the same. One night a barn dance and the next night . . . well, you can see for yourself. That's the beauty of this place . . . you never know what's going to show up. Now you know why I never get bored way out here."

"I don't see Linda anywhere," I said. "What should I do?"

"If she said she was going to be here, then she will be. I suggest you walk around and have a nice time." Then he looked down at my T-shirt and jeans with a frown. "You are underdressed, but the maître d' is a friend of mine, so it should be fine."

Richard walked away and sat down at a table full of people who clearly recognized him. One of the women stood up and gave him a kiss on the cheek, and a man enthusiastically held out his hand. I turned around and decided to walk to the other side of the room, hoping to meet Linda along the way. There were at least 200 people present, and more were walking in every minute. It was hard to recognize any of the details of the barn structure, but as I examined the walls, I noticed that it was the same rough surface. Otherwise the room was elegant and well decorated.

I had nearly reached the opposite side when I felt a tug on my arm.

"Hello," a woman said who was sitting at one of the tables. "Do you remember me? I was serving drinks last night. You were here with your wife."

"Yes, I do. It's nice to see you again. I was just looking for her. Have you seen . . ."

"Oh, I'm sure she'll be here soon. Why don't you have a seat and wait with us. I'll keep a lookout for her while we chat."

I sat down in the open seat and looked around at the others who were eating appetizers and sipping wine. Three of the people were around fifty, but the other five were no more than thirty years old. The woman I met the previous night, whose name was Martha, was at least sixty years old, which seemed to be out of the ordinary for the gathering. I deduced that people had the ability to choose their age, and most chose to be young and vibrant. Then I considered the possibility that it may have more to do with the age they were happiest when they were alive. This thought had just entered my mind when Martha leaned over and spoke into my ear.

"That's more like it," she said, reading my thoughts. "When I was around fifty I remarried and was happier than I had ever been before. His name is Marcus, and he's still on your side in Beaverton. Pretty soon he'll be over here, and I'll be able to see him again, but for now I'm having a grand old time coming to this wonderful barn."

"I'm a little confused," I said. "You remember your husband? I thought you aren't able to carry memories like that from one side to the other. That's what Linda told me."

"Oh, that's true for the most part, but every once in a while we're able to piece things together, and a few memories come. In fact, I was wondering if you might take a message back with you . . . let him know that I'm here waiting for him."

"I'm not sure if I can, to tell you the truth. Wouldn't that be breaking some kind of rule?"

"Oh, there are no rules," she said with a laugh. "No one here would mind."

"I would mind," a man said from the other side of the table. He was tall and had black, slicked-back hair, and had obviously been listening to our conversation. "Just because you're able to remember someone doesn't mean you have the right to send them messages. There are reasons we can't remember what happened before or who we were with before we died. They have to find their own way here in their own time. If you send a message back with him, it might disrupt things. Is that what you want?"

"Oh, Henry, you're overreacting," Martha said to him. "It's not going to hurt anyone if I send him one little message. It's not like I'm going to divulge any secrets."

"And what if he comes here looking for you?" another man said who found himself caught up in the argument. "What if this nice young man tells him about the barn, and you're not here that night. Then we're the ones who will have to deal with him, not you. No one comes here unless they're guided to come. That's how it works and you know it."

It was strange being called a *nice young man* by someone who was half my age. The man who spoke was perhaps twenty-five, but I guessed that he had been much older when he had died. I turned to him and asked, "Who guides us to come here . . . is it God?"

"You act as if God is this guy who sits somewhere up on a cloud telling people what to do," he said. "It doesn't work that way at all. Of course it's God, but then again, everything is God. If you feel moved to speak to a person or you feel guided to go somewhere you've never gone before, that's God, but what Martha's doing is something else. She wants to get him here for her own purposes, not God's."

"And how are you able to tell the difference?" she argued, obviously upset by the whole topic. "For all you know, God told me to tell this nice man to pass the message on. How would you know?"

"I have an idea," I said, wanting to calm the table down before it went any further. "I'll think about it, and if I feel guided to do something, then I'll let you know. That way it won't be you but me who follows through on what I feel."

"I think that's the perfect solution," Martha said, relieved. "If you feel guided, you let me know and I'll give you his address. He's a very nice man. I think you'd like him very much."

Just then I looked toward the door where people from the other side entered the barn, and I saw her. Linda was standing there looking at me, her long white gown brushing against the floor with the light from behind framing her body, making her appear more like an angel than a woman. She held a small white purse in one hand with pearls embedded in the silver handle, and a single thin braid rested alongside her delicate face. She reminded me of how she looked the day we met, when I first saw her in her sister's apartment and felt the energy rush through my body. I had known in that instant that I would marry her and that she would be the most significant woman in my life. And there I was, twenty-five years later on the other side of Heaven, watching her enter the room a vision of elegance and beauty, looking no different than she did that first night.

I excused myself and walked to meet her. Linda didn't move, and never took her eyes off me. I felt like I was floating through the air as I approached. When I arrived, she held out her hand and took a step closer.

"It's nice to see you again," she said. "I'm sorry I'm late, but . . . well, it's kind of hard to explain."

"You don't need to explain anything. I'm just glad you're here."

"Hello, my friends." The maître d' stood next to us holding two menus. "I'm told that this is a very special evening, and a mutual friend has asked that I find a private table where you can speak in low voices and exchange intimate glances." He said these last few words in a voice that resembled Peter Lorre, almost as if we were in a scene from *Casablanca*. I looked and saw Richard raising his glass to us.

"Yes, that would be perfect," I said. "Linda, is that okay with you?"

"That's what I was hoping for," she said without taking her eyes off me. "There's so much I need to talk you about . . . a private table is great."

"Then please follow me," the maître d' said, and we walked around the other tables until we were nearly in the far corner. There were only four small tables there with settings for two, and yet none of the others were occupied. The maître d' pulled out the chair for Linda and helped her get seated, and I sat down on my own. He then handed us both menus, bowed slightly, and walked away.

"This is really beautiful, isn't it?" Linda leaned toward

me as if she didn't want anyone else to hear. "I wish I'd known about this barn before now. I almost feel like I should help keep it a secret so it doesn't become too crowded."

"Is that possible?" I asked. "Does it work in Heaven the same as it does here?"

"Well, in some ways . . . yes. There are many souls that would love to come here and feel like they used to feel. We all have memories of when we were happiest on Earth, and this is the place we can relive them. Look around you . . . isn't it amazing how happy everyone is? It's because this place is so unusual. That's why it isn't exactly advertised, if you know what I mean."

"I'll have to trust you on that," I said, wishing I really did know what she meant. "All I know is that I'm so happy we're here. It's almost petty saying it that way, but I don't know how else to express what I'm feeling. I guess since last night I've started getting used to the idea that there really is a place between Heaven and Earth where miracles like this happen. All I want is to be able to stay here and talk to you."

"You'll be able to stay here as long as you're meant to," she said, leaning back again. "I wish I could say something more, but that's how it works. It's a great gift to come here at all, but it's not the kind of thing you can do forever. You still have a life to lead, and so many things to do before you come back. Then who knows? Maybe you'll be able to hang out in the barn like we do."

"Do you have any idea what I'm supposed to do?" I asked, hoping that living in Heaven gives one psychic abilities.

"Yes, I do," she said, leaning forward again. "You're going to develop a machine that lets people fly through the air. They're going to call it . . . an airplane." She laughed so hard that the table shook. " Of course I don't know what you're supposed to do. No one knows that, except maybe . . ."

"God?"

"Yes, maybe God. But then again, you're going to do an infinite number of things because it's not limited like you think. Remember what I said last night about multiple universes and timelines?"

"You mean the fact that in one reality the car went over the cliff and in the other it didn't?"

"Exactly. That means that there are aspects of you that live one adventure and other aspects that do something completely different. That's because we live in a universe that's dynamic and unlimited. Nothing moves in straight predictable lines, just like this place where we're having dinner right now."

"I was amazed when I walked in here tonight and discovered this restaurant," I said. "It's like something you'd see in a 1940s movie."

"For many of these people, that was a time in their lives when they were happiest, so this is how it manifests. If it were up to me, it would be a little different."

"Any ideas?"

"Well, since I don't remember specifics from my life, it's hard to say, but I would love for this to be a cabana next to the ocean, or maybe a cruise ship."

"Those were both things you loved when you were alive. You started working for a company that specializes in cruises because you and Angela went on one and you loved it so much. That's what led you to become a travel agent a year or so later. So, that means that although you don't remember the details of your life, the things that you loved are still inside you."

"Makes sense," she said. "I'm tempted to ask you more about what things were like, but another part of me doesn't really want to know."

"Why, would it be a problem?" I asked. "I understand that you're only focused on what is happening right *now*, but what would it hurt learning a bit more about what things were like before?"

"I guess it wouldn't," she said. "Okay, so tell me about when we got married. I think that's something I'd like to hear."

"Well, I think I need to back up a little so you'll understand." I took a deep breath, knowing the story would be long. "The first thing you need to know is that I used to be a monk. I entered a monastery when I was eighteen but only stayed for a couple of years. I left to finish college, and because I needed to grow up more before making such a huge decision. We met right after I graduated. I hadn't even been in a relationship before, and we fell in love almost instantly. We were together for about a year when the thoughts about being in the monastery started coming back."

"What does any of this have to do with our getting married?" she asked.

"Don't worry, I'm getting to that. You need to understand the backstory first."

"Okay, go on."

"So I decided I needed to figure out which I really wanted—to get married to you or go back to being a monk. It was such a hard decision, and I didn't want to make a mistake. I decided to spend three months at the monastery praying for guidance, and you were actually really supportive of the idea. I guess you wanted me to be sure, and decided that this would be a good test. Anyway, we didn't sleep together for at least a month before I left because I didn't want it to be even more difficult if I decided not to come back. But then the night came before I was to leave. We went out for an expensive dinner, went for a carriage ride downtown, then . . . well, you know."

"We slept together."

"We sure did," I continued. "It was probably the greatest and most passionate experience of my life. The next day I was off and knew I wouldn't hear from you till I made a decision."

"Why was that?" she asked me.

"The only rule they imposed was that I couldn't have any communication with you while I was there. I guess they felt I needed to make a clean break before I could discern the direction I was being guided. I agreed even though I really didn't like it."

"I have a feeling I didn't like it either."

"You didn't, but once again you were so understanding. Anyway, I was there for about a month praying for a sign and asking God what I was supposed to do . . . until one day a call came in from you."

"I called you? I thought I wasn't allowed to."

"You weren't, and that's why I was so surprised. When I got on the phone I reminded you that I wasn't supposed to have any contact. That's when you told me . . ."

"I think I can see where this is going," she said with a smile.

"You told me that I had received my sign . . . you were pregnant. That's how I found out. I left a day or two later and came back, and a few months later we were married. And that's how Angela came into the world."

"Was it a big wedding?" I could see by the look in her eyes that she hoped it was.

"No, it wasn't big, but it was beautiful. It was an intimate event, and I can remember nearly every detail."

Linda reached over and took my hand. "Show me, then. I want to see my wedding. I didn't think I would be so curious, but I am. I'll probably never have this chance again."

"You want to see through my eyes like you did yesterday?" I asked, excited to experience it again myself.

"Yes, I want to watch the whole thing just like it happened. Can you do that for me?" She looked at me with such hope and vulnerability that I couldn't say no if I wanted to. The idea of guiding her to one of the happiest days of my life was almost too wonderful to be true. I reached across the table and took her other hand.

"I'm really excited to see this with you," I said. "Do I just look into your eyes like I did yesterday?"

"Just look into my eyes and relax. You don't have to do anything but let your mind slow down and release its grip on everything you see here. Nothing will change . . . it'll all still be here when we get back."

I swallowed and took a deep breath, then let my eyes settle on hers. At first nothing seemed to be happening except for the obvious fact that I was staring into the eyes of the woman I'd loved and lost, but then I could feel the tension and the sucking sensation that seemed to pull me out of my body and into a vast open space. I drifted there for a moment, feeling as if I had no control over where we were heading. Then I felt a sensation as if we were beginning to descend, and as if emerging from the clouds, I saw the city below.

CHAPTER FOURTEEN

We hovered above the busy street for a few seconds, and I looked around hoping to see something familiar. It seemed we were in the near north area, perhaps Chicago Avenue, though I still wasn't sure. Then I looked farther down the street and saw a yellow Firebird moving in our direction, and I instantly knew what was happening. It was the car belonging to Renato, my college roommate and best man; and when it pulled up to the curb and both doors opened, I saw Renato and myself emerge.

"We still have an hour," he said to me as we walked toward the glass door of a seven-story loft building. "There's plenty of time to get ready and be there in time."

I was dressed in a white suit and thin black tie while Renato was still in jeans and a T-shirt. We were on the way to the courthouse where the wedding would take place, and I was worried about the time. The scene was vague in my memory, but as I watched it all started coming back to me.

"I can't believe you're not ready yet," the younger Jimmy said as they walked into the building. I hovered above and behind them, following as they entered the elevator. "My parents are going to be waiting, and I can't be late. I can't be late for my own wedding."

"Relax," he said, far more relaxed than I was. "No one's going to be there this early, so we have plenty of time. The courthouse is only about a mile away, and we don't have to worry about parking since we're going to take a cab. Give me fifteen minutes and I'll be ready."

I leaned against the back of the elevator and sighed.

"Man, I'm freaking out," I said. "I didn't think I was going to be this nervous. It's not like I'm having second thoughts or anything, but damn, I just can't seem to calm down. Do you think I'm doing the right thing by getting married? I mean, that fact that she's pregnant and everything . . ."

"I thought you said you're not having second thoughts," Renato said as the door slid open. "And yes, I do think you're making the right decision. To tell you the truth, I think she's too good for you. If she wasn't pregnant she probably wouldn't show up herself."

I would have been offended if I didn't know him. Renato had been one of my best friends since the day we became roommates at Loyola in 1981, immediately after I left the monastery. I had gone from the sheltered life of a seminarian and monk to the wild exploits of living in a dorm. Renato was always at the center, guiding each adventure with expertly honed skill, and that didn't stop after leaving school. We lived together in a huge downtown loft for several months where the party never seemed to end. He was the type of person who could say anything to anyone, no matter how coarse or offensive, and get away with it. It might have been the result of being born and raised just off Chicago's famous Rush Street, or even his Italian heritage. Whatever it was, Renato was the first person I thought of when choosing a best man, and regardless of how things appeared at the moment, I knew he would get me there in time.

"Just get dressed and I'll try to relax," I said to him. "To tell you the truth, I wouldn't mind walking if we have time. I think the exercise would help me focus and calm down. How long would that take?"

"Maybe twenty minutes . . . but that might be pushing it some."

"Not if you hurry. I need do something to get rid of these nerves, and walking would really help."

Ten minutes later we were walking out the door and heading toward the Loop. We walked south on Clark until we crossed the river, then several more blocks till we arrived at Daley Center. That was the meeting spot, ground zero where one family would converge with another, and then the knot would finally be tied. The fact that the wedding was taking place at the courthouse and not a Catholic church was already a major source of disappointment for my mother. It was the advice given by one of my Franciscan friends—get legally married then see how things go. As I floated above and behind Renato and my younger self, I wondered if it had been the right move after all. Perhaps it would have locked my consciousness in place to a greater degree, slowing my wandering impulse and keeping me in place. I could feel Linda's influence gently nudging me past the thought, keeping me focused on what was happening right in front of us.

I saw the famous Picasso sculpture on the far side of the plaza as we crossed Washington, then walked diagonally toward the opposite side. Most of the lunch crowd had already returned to the buildings and skyscrapers that surrounded the Plaza, leaving a smattering of tourists and others wandering about or staring at the giant lion-like monument that had emerged from the mind of the great Spaniard. In the distance I saw my younger brother, Kenny, waving to us. He was twelve at the time, and it was so strange seeing him as a child again. Behind him my parents were standing beside my two sisters, Lisa and Karen, while my older brother Todd stood gazing at the Picasso.

"There they are," I said to Renato. "There's no turning back now."

"There was no turning back from the moment you got me involved," he said. "I'm not going to let you make the worst mistake of your life."

The words seemed to cut through me as I watched them cross the Plaza. It wasn't for that moment that I was sad, but for the future none of them knew about. Who could have predicted that two years later the dream would grind to a resolute halt and that I would spend the next decade trying to overcome my misstep? I looked around the Plaza hoping to see Linda, believing that the sight of her would pull me out of my sudden rush of melancholy. She was nowhere to be found. It was only then that I heard, or perhaps felt, her voice, emanating from somewhere deep within.

"Just trust everything you see," she seemed to be saying to me. "Everything has led to this—you and I watching this together. Don't forget that this is the only moment that matters . . . and I'm with you right now."

I watched Kenny run up to Renato and me, and the sadness suddenly evaporated. He didn't seem to want to wait for us to walk the entire distance across the plaza, and his excitement reminded me that I was about to witness one of the greatest memories of my life.

"Linda's not here yet," Kenny said when he arrived. "So far we're the only ones. Mom's freaking out, by the way. We've been trying to calm her down, but nothing works."

"What is she freaking out about?" I asked him, knowing full well what the answer would be.

"Everything," he said to me. "You're the first kid to get married, it's not in a church, we're in downtown Chicago . . ."

"I get the picture," I said. "How about Dad? Is he okay?"

"He's fine. Mom's the one to worry about."

We arrived at the spot where everyone waited, and I could tell from looking at my mother that Kenny was right. I also knew that it had little to do with what I thought at the time. She always loved Linda and was thrilled we were getting married. Yes, she would have preferred it to be in a church and yes, downtown Chicago scared her, but what was really eating away at her was the fact that it was a priest who told us we should get married at the courthouse. For her it was a kind of betrayal, and even though she didn't know that man, it was something she would hold on to for many years. I was just happy the priest had decided not to come to the wedding. That would have been disastrous.

"When does Linda get here?" Lisa asked. Both of my sisters were standing together near a stone bench not far from the Picasso, and once again it was surreal seeing them so young.

"I'm not sure," I said. "I thought she would have been here by now." I looked at my watch. "We're supposed to be inside in ten minutes, so I hope it isn't too long."

Renato caught my attention and motioned me to look in the opposite direction. I turned around and saw three women, with Linda in the center, walking toward us at a deliberate pace. Linda was holding a small bouquet of flowers, while her sister, Colleen, and her best friend, Deana, walked on either side. Hovering above the scene, I had a sensation like my knees going weak, even though I was definitely without a body at the moment. Linda radiated in a way I had never seen before, or perhaps never noticed. Her black and white dress fit well enough to reveal the presence of the final member of the wedding party— Angela. From my vantage point above the scene, I looked down with such love and joy that it was hard to contain myself. I felt Linda's presence break through and grab my attention.

"I look so beautiful," she said in my mind. "That's what I looked like when I was married?"

"I'll never forget this moment," I said to her. "It wasn't the big wedding most women dream of, but it was *our* moment. We seem to never appreciate moments like these when they're right in front of us, but looking back now, I realize that it was one of the happiest of my life."

"I got lost and parked about two blocks away," a voice said from behind. I turned around and saw Linda's father, Neal, walking toward us. He was a handsome man with broad shoulders and a wide smile. He was about to give his daughter away, and he seemed ready for anything.

"Hi, Dad," Linda said as she gave him a kiss on the cheek. "I was just wondering where you were. We're about to go inside."

"Sorry I was late," he said, then stepped toward my

father and shook his hand. "Is everyone as excited as I am?"

"We're all pretty excited," my mother said, finally releasing her resentment and entering the moment with the rest of us.

"Okay, then let's get my sister married," Colleen said, and with that we crossed the plaza and walked into the building.

Minutes later we were standing outside a large wooden door waiting for the moment to arrive. I never considered that it would be quite so well organized, one couple leaving while the next waited to enter. I stood holding Linda's hand, which was delicate and warm; and my older self could sense the energy, even from my vantage point near the ceiling. The happiness I felt in that moment was not darkened by the breakdowns and disappointments to be experienced later in life, nor was it dimmed by the struggle to mature and still keep the marriage strong. Two people who were in love stood praying they had what it took to make it work, that they would find the courage to weather whatever storms lay ahead. I hated the advantage I had from above knowing how it would all turn out. It felt unfair that I would be there at all, though there was nowhere in the world I would rather be.

The door opened and another happy couple was led into the hall. They were younger than Linda and I, but their glow was no less dim. A woman in her mid-fifties said goodbye then turned her attention to us.

"You must be the Twymans," she said as she looked down at her clipboard. "We're so happy to share this experience with you. Why don't you come inside and we'll begin."

We followed her into the room that was filled with dark

wood and the scent of flowers. A roundish man stood at the far side with thinning hair and a red complexion, and he motioned with his eyes for us to join him there. Linda let go of my hand and went to stand by her sister and Deana, while Renato came and stood at my side. The others in the room seemed to find their places, and when all were settled in, the judge began.

"I'd like to welcome all of you to this important ceremony. James Twyman and Linda Murphy have chosen to enter into a sacred commitment, and as a representative of the court, I am here to oversee their vows."

I looked at Linda, who was standing to my left. She was staring straight ahead as if she didn't want to miss a single word, absorbing everything the judge said. The others stood as if they were intruders, unsure if they really belonged to such a strange and wonderful moment. I let my own mind relax and returned to the ceremony unfolding in front of me.

"I'm told that the bride and groom have written their own vows," he continued, "and so I'd like to allow them to express those promises to one another before everyone present."

I swallowed and turned to face Linda, and as she turned toward me I took hold of her hand. Her eyes were so deep and moist with life, and at first I thought I would lose myself in them, unable to remember what I had written and memorized. Then she smiled, and the words flooded into my mind. I began to speak as if from another room, removed yet so intimately present.

"Linda, I wish I could express how much this moment means to me. I remember the night I met you and we shared our first conversation and kiss. I went home that night knowing I had met the woman I would someday marry, the woman I hoped I would spend the rest of my life with. There was no way I could have known just how wonderful you were or how lucky I was to have won your heart. But now I do know, and that's why I'm so amazed to be standing here with our families looking on as I give myself to you without reserve. I promise that I will love you till the day I die, and will never stop even after death. I promise that I will provide for you and give everything I have to support you and our family. And most of all, I promise that I will never forsake you but will stand beside you as one who understands and demonstrates just how lucky he is, and I'll never forget to remind you that you're the most precious gift in the world to me. There's nothing that can equal this moment, or every other moment that will come after this one as we build a life together."

I listened to the words my younger self spoke from a perspective I never imagined I would possess. Linda began to speak her vows to me, but I was so lost in the emotions that were swimming through my spirit that I could hardly hear her over my own inner exchange. I meant every one of those words when I spoke them, but I didn't have the fortitude to withstand the tremors of responsibility and life, and in the end I did fail her. I had promised to stand beside her even in death, and here I was doing just that.

Linda was within me watching the whole scene through my eyes, feeling the love and sensing my own regret. And I had the feeling that she was holding my hand, just as our counterparts were holding hands below. It filled me with an air of devotion that I didn't expect and didn't want to deny. I drank it in, like one dying of thirst, and let it soothe my soul in a way I desperately needed to be soothed.

The judge, noticing we had finished, looked around the room and said, "Then it is my privilege to confirm this marriage, and my honor to introduce you to Mr. and Mrs. James Twyman."

As everyone in the room began to clap, Linda and I turned around to finally face them. In the same instant, I felt myself being pulled higher over the group, and as if I was being ripped through the ceiling, the scene disappeared and I felt myself being engulfed by white clouds. I tried to resist the pull and remain there, but they were already gone, and seconds later I felt myself fall into my body in the barn.

CHAPTER FIFTEEN

I opened my eyes and saw Linda looking straight at me. I tried to turn away, but the force of her energy was too much to resist. The sound of the restaurant suddenly reminded me where we were, in a barn in the middle of a magical forest where Heaven and Earth somehow blend into one world. In that moment, after watching one of the greatest moments of my life and knowing every detail that followed, I felt my heart being filled with terrible guilt. It started off so well, with so much life and beauty, but it wore off so quickly. If I had only known then what became so apparent with the passing of time, I would have made very different decisions that would have changed both of our lives.

"That was our wedding," she said to me. "It was more beautiful than I imagined it would be."

"Yes, it was," I said, then bowed my head slightly. "It began with such promise, until I threw it all away two years later."

"What do you mean when you say that you threw it all away?" she asked.

"I was completely naïve at the time," I told her. "We

were so young when we got married, and my life had no real direction. All I knew was that I wanted to do something big, something that would make an impact on the world. That was not of much interest to you. You wanted to raise a family and have a good marriage, but I wanted to write books and make movies . . ."

"It sounds like you did those things."

"I did, but look what it cost me. There had to be a way I could do those things and still save our marriage. Instead, I started to lose interest, and I uprooted everything. We moved to Oregon because I decided we needed to be on the West Coast, and that's where we separated. I realized the mistake I made almost immediately, but you were so hurt. I tried for so many years to save the marriage, but you were never really able to open your heart to me again."

"Are you sure that's true?" she asked me.

"What do you mean? Do you realize that we were separated for over ten years before we actually got divorced? That's because I didn't want it. I thought that someday you'd realize that I had changed and would want me back. It actually seemed to be working, even though it took so many years. You were thinking about moving out to Oregon when you were killed. You thought that you were going to be laid off from your job in a few months and said you wanted to be with Angela and me. I knew that if you did that, then everything would change. You would need me to get settled and you would see once and for all that we should be together."

"But it never happened, right?"

"No, it never happened."

"So, why do you think you're here, then?" she asked as if she already knew the answer.

"That's what I'm trying to figure out. You told me that I needed to learn something, otherwise I wouldn't have been able to find this place. I just wish I knew what it was."

"I think you do know what it is," she said. "You just haven't found the courage to see it yet."

Martha suddenly appeared at our table and looked as if she had something important to say.

"Hello, Linda . . . it's so nice to see that you found your way back. And Jimmy . . . that's your name, right?"

"Yes, that's my name."

"I know that you shouldn't go and find my husband, but just in case you do feel called to do so, I thought I would give you a little information." She looked over her shoulder to make sure no one else at her table could hear her. "I want you to tell him to look in the butterfly drawer . . . that's all. He won't believe you at first, but if you tell him that, it'll make all the difference in the world."

"I'm not sure if I'm supposed to . . ."

"Like I said, only if you feel *guided* to do so." Then she gave me a wink and walked away.

"Do I want to know what that was about?" Linda asked.

"Probably not . . . it's just a little secret I have with Martha."

The waiter walked up to our table and smiled. "Good evening . . . I'm so happy to be able to serve you tonight. I wish we had a larger selection to offer, but we are a bit limited at the moment."

I looked at the menu, but the inside was blank.

"There isn't anything here," I said. "Did something get misplaced . . ."

"No, sir, that's the menu we have every night . . . which

means that anything you order we can make."

"But you just said that you were a bit limited."

"Well, we are limited if you take into consideration your own past experience. You see, the only dishes you would be able to order are the ones you've either had or have heard of. Now, I know that you're a guest, which means that you're able to remember a great deal more than most people here, but the result is the same. Regardless of how much you know, there is still a great deal more that you do not. In that way, we are all a bit limited."

"What he's trying to say is that if you're limited, we're all limited," Linda said to me. "That's because we see each other slightly differently from how we might see ourselves. What happens to one happens to all . . . do you understand?"

"That's correct, ma'am," said the waiter. "In this case we're both limited because I cannot think of or prepare what you do not order, and you cannot order what you do not know. It's really quite simple."

"Okay," I said to Linda, "maybe I should just follow your lead and just order whatever you decide. That way we'll both be safe."

"But that's not exactly true because I really don't have a reference for food like I used to. It's not something we often do here. I think we'll just do whatever everyone else does and eat whatever he brings us. I hear it's always the best choice."

"Very well, ma'am," he said with a nod. "I won't disappoint you. And to drink?"

"We'll have whatever you decide," I said to him.

"You catch on very fast, sir. Well done." The waiter took our menus and walked away.

"That was one of the most interesting interactions I've ever had with a waiter," I said to her.

"Don't worry, you'll get used to it. Now, we were in the middle of something before . . . do you remember what it was?"

"You said that I already know what I'm here for, but I'm afraid to admit it."

"Yes, now I remember. What do you think of that?"

"I'm not sure, to tell you the truth. I really don't know what it is. I thought I was here because I missed you and God was giving me a way to heal my grief."

"That may be true," she said, "but it isn't a lesson. Try to go a little deeper."

"Am I here to learn what happened to you so we can find the men who were involved? Wait, don't even answer because I know what you're going to say. That has nothing to do with me, right? Whatever lesson I'm here to learn, it's something that's very personal."

"I couldn't have said it better myself."

The waiter appeared with two large goblets filled with a red-tinted liquid.

"I've brought something I think you'll like very much," he said. "Please, ma'am, you be the first to try."

Linda took a sip and her eyes lit up. "Wow, this is wonderful. I love it."

Then I took a sip from my glass and had a very different experience. "You're kidding," I said. "This isn't good at all . . . it tastes like an inexpensive blush."

"Red Zinfandel," he said. "I was sure that it was the lady's choice."

"Well, I don't know about him, but I think it's great," she said.

The waiter walked off feeling vindicated.

"This is too funny," I said to her. "Last night we had one of the finest chardonnays I've ever tasted, and I thought that that was just how things work here. Tonight they serve the exact wine you would have loved when you were alive. I could never understand why you liked that stuff."

"I like it because it's so fruity and sweet," she said. "How can you say that it's not good? You're just pretending not to like it."

"I have to say that tonight it's the finest glass of wine I've ever had, simply because I'm having it with you."

We brought our glasses together for a toast.

"Before we drink, what should we toast?" Linda asked.

I thought about it for a moment, wondering what would be appropriate given the extraordinary circumstances of the event. Would it be right for us to toast to being together again, or that such magic was still present in the world? As I was thinking about it, the obvious answer came into my mind.

"Let's toast to every lesson being learned, and every opportunity being joyfully received," I said.

"I can live with that," Linda responded, and we brought our glasses together again, but before she took a sip, Linda said, "I think we should leave the lesson issue alone for a bit. You'll know what it is when the time is right."

"Sounds good to me," I said. "Besides, I would rather enjoy having a beautiful dinner with my wife, something I never thought I would be able to do again."

"I thought you said I was your ex-wife," she said to me. "Why don't you say that?"

I set my glass down on the table and swallowed. "You know, that's something you used to say to me a lot. I never really stopped calling you my wife. It's partly because I always wanted to be married to you. The other part is a bit deeper, I think, especially later. I guess that after you died certain people wondered if I was as affected as others were. Clearly I didn't lose a mother or a daughter or a sister, but it was the hardest thing I've ever had to go through. I felt like I lost a wife, regardless of whether we were still married. That didn't matter to me. What did matter was that I felt the loss so deeply and it makes it easier to call you my wife. I hope that doesn't bother you."

"I think it's beautiful," she said. "I just wanted to understand why. You know, I feel like I'm just getting to know you, and you have a pretty big advantage. You may feel familiar to me, but I don't remember any of this. But I do feel affection toward you, which tells me that I must have loved you as well."

"That feels really good to hear," I said. "I always wondered if you did."

"And now I can love you in an even deeper way. I'm not bound by the same emotions I was on Earth. Now I can see you in a way that defies all those limitations, and love you for who you are in truth . . . just like God does."

"You said that yesterday as well, but I'm not sure I know what you mean."

"It means that I can love you without conditions," she said. "That's the highest love there is, and that's why I say that it's the same as the love of God. God doesn't love us for what we've done or who we may someday become. God loves us because we were created perfect, and what God creates perfect remains perfect no matter what happens."

"I do understand that," I said, "at least intellectually. But it's still hard for me to see how God, or you for that matter, can see past the terrible things many of us have done in our lives. Isn't there any kind of punishment or retribution?"

"We were created in the image of God, and we've been trying to repay God for the favor ever since," she said, smiling at her joke.

"What does that mean?"

"The Bible says that we were created in the image of God, right? Well, it's also true that we created God in our image, at least the way we see God. That's why so many of the images we write in stories and everywhere else tell us more about who *we* are than who God is. In many religions, God is a vindictive old man who is quick to punish, and is always looking for a reason to cast us into hell. That sounds like a lot of people in the world more than it sounds like God. I can tell you that it doesn't work like that at all. God is all-forgiving and is the very essence of love. Most of us were raised with this Santa Claus image . . . an old man in the sky writing down our sins. Think about that for a moment and tell me if it makes any sense at all. Isn't it more likely that the picture Jesus gave us was more accurate, a God that loves us and drops everything to find us when we're afraid and lost?"

"But what about someone who does something that destroys others' lives?" I asked. "Let's take a mass murderer, or Hitler."

"Always go for the worst case."

"Yes, why not? I still can't see how a person like that just gets to walk away guilt free. There has to be some kind of accountability."

"Well, if you look over at the bar," she said, "you'll see

Hitler having a drink with Gandhi. That should tell you something."

I spun around to see what she meant. There was no one who resembled either of those men at the bar.

"Was that a joke?" I asked her.

"Of course it was," she said with a wide smile. "Gandhi would never have a drink with Hitler because he never drank alcohol. How could you fall for that?"

"I didn't think you had any memory of people or places on the other side," I said to her. "How do you even know who Hitler and Gandhi are?"

She took a sip of her blush. "That's easy. There are certain people and events that are so engrained in the mass consciousness that everyone knows them, no matter which side of the veil they're on. I know who John Lennon is, Michael Jackson . . ."

"How's he doing, by the way?"

"Took him a little while to adjust, but now he's fine."

The waiter stepped up carrying two plates of food.

"And here we are," he said. "For the lady I've brought a lovely salmon cooked in a zesty lemon sauce, and for you, sir . . ."

He set the plate in front of me. It was a large hamburger with fries and a pickle. I looked up, and he smiled down on me.

"Hamburger?" I said. "I should have mentioned that I'm a vegetarian."

"Yes, I am aware, sir, but I think you'll find that everything is different here, including meat. Try it and tell me what you think."

I picked up the burger and took a bite. I was stunned by the taste, the most amazing and tantalizing food I had ever tasted. It was meat, but it wasn't at the same time. I didn't know how to react.

"It's incredible," I said. "Is it meat . . . like, from a cow?"

"No sir, no cows were killed to make that burger. Let's just say that it's something I knew you missed, so I made sure that it was made with a very special recipe."

"Well, thank you very much," I said. The waiter bowed and walked away.

"You seem really preoccupied with thoughts of guilt," Linda said as she cut into her salmon. "Do you have any idea why?"

I thought about the question and considered what she said. Was I really obsessed with the topic? If I was, then maybe she was right . . . perhaps this was a clue to what I had come to learn.

"I guess I've been preoccupied with it since you were killed," I said. "For the longest time we had no idea who or why . . . then all of a sudden I hear that someone confessed, and that the man hasn't even been charged because they want to make sure he isn't making it up. I was enraged, both because he admitted to doing it and because now there was this other question. I want whoever did this to pay for how they took your life. Is that really so hard for you to understand?"

"It's not hard to understand at all," she said. "I'm sure you also don't want them out running around so they won't hurt anyone else . . . is that right?"

"Yes, that is right."

"And you probably also want them to have the chance to learn that what they did was wrong so their souls can grow . . . is that correct?"

I stopped and thought for a moment.

"Yes, I guess that's true as well, but mainly I want them to be caught and be held responsible."

"And what, other than saving people from their violence, does that help?"

"I'm not sure," I said, starting to get confused. "I do want them to have the chance to be rehabilitated, but I really want them to . . ."

"Yes, I understand," she said. "You want them to pay. Okay, let me ask you one more question. If you were God, what do you think you would say to those men? Do you think you would strike them down, or would you offer them something else?"

"I'm not sure what you're asking," I said, trying to avoid the point I knew she was making.

"What would you do if you were God? Remember that we already agreed that God is all-loving and all-forgiving. Those men are God's children just like we are. So if you imagined yourself to be God right now, and those men were right here in front of us, what would you say to them?"

I closed my eyes and imagined what she said. First I imagined that I was God, then I pictured two men in front of me who were responsible for Linda's death. To my great surprise, I felt love for them. I didn't see two murderers, but two children who were wounded and hurt to the point that they didn't understand right from wrong. They had tears in their eyes as if they suddenly realized what they had done. Then I opened my eyes and looked back at Linda.

"I would say that I love them, and that I forgive them."

I couldn't believe that the words came out of my mouth. Moments earlier I wanted to take them in my hands and strangle them both, and now all I was feeling was profound love.

"This is the difference between the mind and the heart," she said. "The mind needs to arrange things and judge them according to its own ideas and history. The heart simply opens and loves, and that's what God does. It's what we're all called to do as well. If we can only realize that everything that ever happens is actually leading us to a greater experience of love and forgiveness, then we begin to understand that we are one with God and cannot be separated. Then everything changes and we respond in new and very holy ways."

"So these are the lessons you learn in Heaven," I said to her.

"They don't need to be learned just in Heaven. You can learn them anytime and anywhere. That's why I said that Heaven is all around us, just like divinity is all around us as well."

We sat and finished our meals and talked about less important things. It felt wonderful to be able to sit together, almost as if no time had passed and nothing terrible ever happened. I didn't know how much time passed, but I realized that people were beginning to walk toward the back door with the light streaming from the other side.

"It looks like it's time for me to go again," she said. "I really wish I didn't have to because I'm really enjoying our time together. If it wasn't against the rules, I'd bring you with me."

"This isn't the last time I'll see you, is it? I don't want to go yet. I feel there's still so much for me to learn."

"There is," she said. "There's so much for all of us to learn. I also don't feel like you've learned the lesson you came to learn quite yet. You're getting closer, but there's still more."

"I don't want to learn too much," I told her, "otherwise this might all suddenly end."

"Nothing ever ends, as you can see." She motioned around her as people moved past us toward the door. "Nothing ever ends because love goes on forever. That's a lesson we all need to learn. That's the lesson Heaven teaches."

Linda stood up from her chair and began walking toward the door with the others. I followed her and took her arm before she got too far.

"Promise you'll come back," I said. "I need to see you again, even if it's just one more time. Please promise."

She smiled and said, "I promise," then kissed me on the cheek. "I'll see you tomorrow night."

Then she turned and walked through the door, and the light suddenly faded away.

CHAPTER SIXTEEN

I woke up the next morning feeling heavy and out-of-sorts. It was as if I was living in a dream, caught between two different worlds and not being able to decide which I wanted to stay in. In one world I was lost in a treacherous forest sleeping in the spare room of the man whose only job was to caretake the bridge between Heaven and Earth, and in the other I was engaged in a profound conversation with the woman I had loved most of my life but had tragically lost three and a half years earlier.

If there was a choice to make, I would definitely choose to stay with her and make the nightly journey to the barn just as the others did. Perhaps there was a way to get Angela to join me, and the three of us could be a family again. On the other hand, I was only a guest at the party, and there was no telling how long I was welcome to stay. Would I end up being like the woman who tried to stay even after she was meant to leave? As I lay there in bed, my mind was filled with more questions than answers, and I wondered what I would decide.

Richard knocked on my door, and the smell of fresh coffee wafted into the room. "Are you awake in there?" he asked. "You can sleep as long as you need to, but I thought I should at least offer you some breakfast."

"I'll be out in a minute," I told him, and throwing off the covers, I shifted my body to a standing position.

"All right, it's ready whenever you are," he said, then walked away.

I put on a fresh shirt that Richard gave me, and wondered if he had heard complaints about how I looked the night before. Not only was I terribly underdressed for the dinner, but I was also beginning to smell. There was a pan of water in the room that I used to wash my face and brush my teeth, then after taking one final breath, I left to start the day.

"What time is it?" I asked him, knowing that my cell phone had long since died, and I had no way of telling time.

"It's after eleven," he said as he poured me a cup of coffee. "I guess it took a lot out of you last night. Don't worry, it's very common. Nearly everyone has that reaction after visiting the barn . . . either that or they get no sleep at all. Hard to tell which way it's going to be."

"Is it really different every night?" I asked as I sat down at the small table and took a sip. "The first night it was a barn dance, and last night it was a plush restaurant. Is that normal?"

"It changes a lot," he explained. "That's one of the reasons why the barn is so popular . . . they never really know what they're going to walk into. Tonight it could be a disco, for all I know."

"God, I hope not," I said, making a sour face. "Who decides what it's going to be?"

"That's a question I've never been able to answer. I guess the only guess I have is God. I know that when they come through the door they have no idea what to expect . . ."

"But how do they choose what to wear if they don't know?" I asked.

"That's the easy part. It's not the same as it would be on this side. Here, you would have to get back in your car, go home, and change. They just imagine how they want to look and that's all. It's also how they decide what age to be and that kind of thing. When you see Linda, you see her when she was in her prime. That's because that's the time when she felt most alive, and it's that aliveness that draws the image into her mind. If she wanted, she could choose a different way of looking, but for the most part the way they show up the first time is how they stay."

"But there were a lot of people who were older," I said. "Why didn't they choose to be young again?"

"What makes you think that that wasn't the time they felt most alive? At the same time, some of them don't realize they have the power to manifest themselves however they choose. It has to do with how mature or experienced they are on a soul level. Sometimes they don't realize they have a choice, so they show up the way they looked when they died. Some of them realize this at some point or another and make a different choice. It doesn't happen very often, but I have seen it before."

"How many times do you think I'll be able to go back?" I asked him. "I know I'm welcome tonight, but after that . . ."

"Impossible to say. Most of the people I've brought here only had one visit, so you're already ahead. The most I ever saw was five, and that was only because the person was really slow." He tried to hide his smile as he said this, but I saw it nonetheless.

"What are you trying to say? If I break his record does that mean that I'm the slowest of them all? I hope I am, if that means I get to keep coming back."

"I'm sorry . . . but you need to remember that I don't get many *living* guests out here. To answer your question, you'll keep being invited back until you learn whatever it is you came to learn. Only you know what that is."

"Linda said that as well, but I don't think I do."

Richard poured granola into a bowl and offered it to me. I looked around wondering if there was any milk to pour over it, then I saw Richard eat his own dry. I followed course and did the same.

"Are you sure about that?" he asked me. "What has been the main topic of your conversation with Linda?"

I thought about that for a moment, and within seconds the answer became abundantly clear.

"We've talked a lot about forgiveness and guilt. I think she's trying to get me to see that forgiveness is the path to healing, and that it's the only way we experience grace. We've also talked a lot about God and how God thinks."

"And how does God think, in your opinion? Be careful how you answer, by the way. You don't want to commit blasphemy or anything. You never know who's listening."

"God thinks in terms of oneness," I said, "which is the same as saying unconditional love. Linda said that we're here to think and act in the same way . . . to imitate God. When we do, we then experience peace and happiness."

Richard smiled and said, "I would say you're learning quite a lot."

"These were things I understood intellectually before, but now it feels like it's gone deeper. Maybe that's what it's all about."

"I like to call that the thirteen-inch journey . . . the journey from the mind to the heart. It's easy to understand a concept intellectually, but if you don't embody it, then it makes no difference in your life. When it sinks into your heart, then everything changes. You begin to live the truth, not just think about it. If that's what you're learning, then I would say you're doing quite well."

"So what's next?" I asked him.

"God only knows, Jimmy . . . and I mean that quite literally."

"That's what I'm counting on tonight. Maybe He'll show up and tell me."

"Or She," he said without looking.

"What do you mean . . . God is a She? And Mexican, I hear."

Richard looked up at me again and smiled. "God is neither He nor She," he explained. "I've always been curious as to why people need God to be one or the other. It's easy to accept that everything is contained within God, but we're so locked in the idea of black and white, male and female, that we forget."

"So let me ask you in a very straightforward way," I said. "Have you seen God? Has God ever come to the barn?"

"I'm seeing God right now," he said without hesitating, "through you. Isn't that the point . . . to be able to perceive the Divine in every situation, and to see God in each person we encounter? My willingness to see it in you means that I'm also open to sensing it within myself. Then the boundaries begin to break down and separation means less and less. As you said before, God sees everything as one, not separate. If we learn to do the same, then maybe everything will change."

"Everything will change," I repeated. "I just don't want anything to change before tonight, if that's okay."

CHAPTER SEVENTEEN

The sun had already set by the time we arrived at the barn. I could hear the talk and laughter from outside and wondered what we were about to walk into.

"Are you ready?" Richard asked as he grabbed hold of the handle.

"As ready as I'm ever going to be," I said.

He opened the door, and of course everything had changed. The restaurant was gone, and in its place was a theater lounge with small tables and a medium-sized stage in front. People were streaming in from the door with the bright light, and many had already reserved their seats at the tables closest to the stage. There was a buzz in the room that hadn't been present the other two nights, and I wondered what everyone was waiting for.

"Is Elvis coming tonight?" I asked Richard.

"No, he stopped coming years ago after an altercation with a barmaid."

I looked to see if he was joking. At first his face didn't betray his intention, but seconds later his smile told me what I needed to know.

"Seriously, do you know what's going to happen?"

"I have no idea," he said. "I'm as lost as you are . . . always am. The only difference between us is that it happens to me every night. I'm used to it. Now, I think I see a beautiful young woman over there trying to get your attention."

I looked in the direction he pointed and saw Linda waving at me, motioning for me to join her at a table in the back of the room.

"I guess that's my cue," I said to him.

"Good luck, Jimmy. Just keep your heart open, and everything will be fine."

I walked over to Linda, and she gave me a familiar hug. It felt as it always did, a feeling I'll never forget as long as I live. I held her an extra second, not wanting it to end.

"I'm so happy you're here," she said as she pulled back and looked into my eyes. "And I'm really excited to see what's going to happen tonight."

"Do you mean between the two of us, or on the stage?"

"Both, actually. I don't know what to expect, but tonight there should be more people than normal. I think most of them know what's going to happen, but I don't."

We sat down at the table Linda chose in the back of the room. I was glad we weren't in the center of the activity since I was far more interested in talking to her than in viewing whatever show was planned. Within seconds the waiter appeared, the same from the previous evening, to take our drink order.

"Will you be having the same as last evening, ma'am?" he asked.

"Yes, that's perfect," she said to him.

"I'll have something different," I said, choosing not to

have the sweet blush Linda loved so much. "Something red, maybe a Malbec or Shiraz."

"Absolutely, sir. I'll be right back with both."

He walked away and I turned back to Linda.

"I've been thinking a lot about our conversation last night," I said. "I think I know what my lesson is."

"Tell me what you think," she said, leaning forward. There was a sparkle in her eyes that almost entranced me. Had it always been there, or was I just now noticing it? It was otherworldly, and yet it seemed so normal and in character. It was as if her soul was no longer hidden from me, and when I looked I saw all of her, not just the limited personality that rests at the surface of most lives. It was invigorating, and I didn't want to look away.

"The one topic that keeps coming up over and over is forgiveness," I said. "I've been so filled with anger over what happened to you, and I haven't been able to let it go. When we didn't know who killed you, it sat there in my gut like a lead weight, then I heard that someone confessed, and I finally had someone to unleash all that hatred on. I think the reason I'm here is to forgive those men. It doesn't mean that I don't want them to be charged and go to jail, but I do know that if I'm ever going to heal, I need to let it go at some point."

"So you think that the lesson has to do with forgiving the men who killed me, is that correct?"

"I think it is. I'm trying to see them in a different way. That's what you've been saying to me, right?"

"Yes it is, and I do agree that it is a part of what you're here for. I'm just not sure if it's the only thing."

The waiter returned with our wine and set each glass in front of us.

"Will there be anything else?" he asked.

"We're fine, thank you," I said.

He walked away and I looked back at Linda.

"You don't think it's the only thing?" I asked. "What more could there be? For over three years we've been waiting and feeling so helpless, especially since we didn't know what really happened. When I found out they had someone, it was like stirring the pot and everything I had pushed down came up to the surface again. But at least I can see that now."

"Once again, I'm not denying that, but there's something else I need you to see—the lesson you need to learn has nothing to do with anyone else. It has to do with you and only you."

"I'm not sure what that even means. What I said does have to do with me . . . it has to do with me forgiving the men who killed you."

"Okay, let me explain it this way," she said. "Even the anger and resentment you feel toward those men has more to do with you than them. They represent something that's inside of you, something you're not willing to look at. It's easier to project your anger at them than realize that it all has something to do with you."

"How could your being killed have anything to do with me?" I asked her.

"Everything you perceive, everything you see, and everything you feel has to do with what's inside you. We all have shadows inside us that we don't want to look at, and we project them onto other people so we don't have to see them. We tell ourselves that it's all out there, not within. But in the end everything is within, and there's nothing we can really change but our own hearts. When we do that, then we aren't affected in the same way . . . we react from a place of compassion rather than attack."

"I'm perfectly justified in being angry at those men, or anyone else who does something that terrible. I can't see how it shows that I'm the one who needs to be healed."

"You need to go deeper, Jimmy. There's something you're not seeing that you need to become aware of. I promise you that it's the reason you're here. When you finally see it clearly, it will all make perfect sense . . . I promise."

A man stepped onto the stage and the house lights slowly dimmed. I turned away from Linda to see what was happening.

"Ladies and gentlemen, I am so happy you could join us tonight for this very special presentation. I know you've been waiting for the show, so I won't take up any more time. Will you please put your hands together and give a very warm welcome to . . . the king of stage hypnosis, Lance DeMille."

Wild applause followed, and a middle-aged man in a long tuxedo stepped onto the stage. His well-trimmed goatee and slick raven black hair made me think of classic magicians from the 1920s, and it was clear that he commanded great respect from everyone in the audience.

"Thank you very much," he said in a deep voice. "I am so happy to be back and have this opportunity to unlock the secrets of the subconscious mind. There is a land of mystery, a whole world of activity, that we are not aware of in our everyday lives that influences every decision we make. It's like a vast ocean and contains more information than our conscious minds could ever dream of, and it's able to process information at speeds that are unbelievable and incomprehensible. And best of all, it is perfectly natural. Hypnosis is not something that happens only when we're in the hands of a skilled practitioner like myself, but throughout our daily lives in the most ordinary circumstances. I would venture to say that we fall under the spell of hypnosis dozens of times a day without realizing it. But tonight we're going to do something very different. Tonight you're going to have the opportunity to join me onstage and experience this phenomenon yourself . . . that is, if you're brave enough."

Applause rang through the barn once again, and I turned back to Linda.

"Do you want to know why this is really amazing to me?" I asked. "We went to a hypnotist the first night we met, remember? We were with your sister and my friend Curtis and we went to a place called Sally's Stage. Do you remember?"

"Of course," she said. "Then we went to the bar . . . Cheers. I was wondering what happened after we left Cheers. Can you tell me about it again?"

"Well, I remember that we left the bar and I walked you to your apartment, which was just a few doors away. I'll never forget that moment because it's where I kissed you for the first time. We stood there in the doorway, and it was so romantic. Then you went inside, but it wasn't long before we were together for good. I moved in a few weeks later, and we lived inside this little tiny studio apartment. It was an amazing time."

"Don't stop," she said. "Just keep saying what comes to your mind."

"What do you mean?" I asked. "You want me to just talk?"

"I want you to tell me what you remember," she said, looking as if she knew what was about to happen next.

"Okay," I said to her, shifting in my seat. "We lived there pretty much until we got married, then we got a bigger place. Angela came along after that, and we were a family. It was the happiest time in my life, and for a couple of years everything went great. Then I started to get really dissatisfied with my job, and I couldn't take it anymore. I decided that we should move out to Oregon and serve the world. I don't know why I had to be so dramatic, but it really tore you apart. In the end we moved, then we separated about a month later."

"We separated after only a month of being in Oregon?" she said.

"Yes, we separated because you didn't really want to be there, but for me it was a new life. I could have saved our marriage if I'd wanted to, but I was so caught up in my own stuff that I didn't know how."

"I want to see it," she said to me.

I was already used to this request, almost expecting it to come. "What do you want to see?" I asked. "Which part?"

"Just let your heart take us to the scene that will teach us the most," she answered, reaching out to take my hand. I looked deep into her eyes just as I had before.

"The part that will teach us the most," I repeated. "I'm not sure when that would be."

"You don't have to know, you just have to trust. Hold my hand and let your body relax. You've done this twice before so it should be easy."

Easy was not the word I would have chosen to describe the experience. Disorienting or bewildering perhaps, but not easy. I took a deep breath and let my gaze soften, then allowed Linda's radiance to envelop me. I realized that there was a faint glow around her, perhaps the result of the white background, and as long as I didn't focus on it the light seemed to increase and pulsate. I also noticed that as it increased, my heart felt buoyant, as if it wanted to float away. I decided not to resist the sensation, but see where it led. Within seconds everything in the barn began to dissolve, and I felt like we were soaring through the clouds. Then we started to descend, and I could see the city landscape below. I looked around expecting to see Chicago, but that didn't appear to be where we were. I couldn't find the Sears Tower, the Hancock, or Lake Michigan. Then I saw a landmark that told me exactly where we were . . . the St. Louis Arch.

Like a silent glider, we soared over the city then turned left, seeming to leave it behind. We crossed the river, which meant we were heading back into Illinois, then began to descend lower. I could see houses and fields in the distance, but nothing I could discern or identify. Then I noticed a large stretch of land with hills and winding drives, as if it was a park or sanctuary. Then I saw what looked like an enormous outdoor arena with a stage and domed roof. Around the base of the stage were swooping stone arms supporting a tall needle-like spike at the very top. At first I was confused and wondered if I had ever been there at all, then with a sudden and disheartening rush it all came back to me.

"Oh my God," I said within myself so she would hear. "I know where this is . . . it's called Our Lady of the Snows, a Catholic shrine outside of St. Louis. But why here?"

"Have we ever been here before?" I felt her ask.

"Yes, we have been there before . . . it's a place I tried to forget. I don't think I can do this. I need to pull back. Please, Linda, don't make me go back there."

"Stay with me," she urged. "If this is where your soul brought us, then there must be a reason."

"There is a reason," I said. "A very big one. And that's why I don't want to be here. I don't want to see it."

But it was too late.

CHAPTER EIGHTEEN

I felt my spirit retract, pulling back on the throttle of my soul in a fruitless attempt to escape. Instead, we drew closer to the massive property as if I had no control, and I felt my heart rate increase beyond healthy levels. I remembered all too well what had happened there twenty years earlier, but hadn't realized how deeply it had ground itself into my consciousness. My insides clenched as if trying to avoid the inevitable descent, then we hovered over a small fountain or pool with what looked like several metal bell sculptures in the center.

"It's Annunciation Garden," I said. "I remember this . . . and I remember when we came here. This is the last place I want to be right now."

"Tell me about it," Linda said to me as we moved past the pool then up the small road that led to several buildings in the distance.

"I was in sales at the time . . . I think it was less than two years after we got married. I was working for this company called Craftmatic . . . selling adjustable beds. I really hated it, but I was really good. I would go into people's homes and high-pressure them into buying. They sent me to St. Louis once to run some appointments, and I thought it would be nice if you and Angela came along. I had been here once before and figured you two could walk around while I was gone. There's a hotel up ahead. I think we're going toward it now."

"But why was that trip significant?" I felt her ask me.

I didn't answer because it meant I would have to admit something that was too difficult to face. Instead, I watched the scene unfold, moving closer to the hotel until I noticed a small blue Ford Escort parked in a lot with a couple opening the front doors to get out. I watched as Linda opened the back door and unsnapped Angela from the child seat. It was amazing to watch my young daughter as she jumped out and stretched, happy to finally be out of the car.

"Mommy," Angela said, "I have to go potty . . . I have to go."

"We'll be inside in a minute," Linda told her as she took Angela's hand. "Your daddy's going to get us checked in, then we'll go to the room so you can use the toilet." Then she turned to me. "I'm exhausted and hungry. Is there anywhere we can get something to eat?"

"I think there's a restaurant right across the street," I told her. "Why don't you guys go there and I'll check us in. She can use the bathroom, then we'll meet in the restaurant."

Linda and Angela walked away from the hotel and crossed the street, and I walked to the office. I felt my older self hovering above the registration desk watching me pay for the room, then cross the street to join the others. They were already sitting down when I walked in.

"It's not too bad, is it?" I asked as I sat down at the table. "There are trails and little shrines all over the place, so when I'm gone the two of you can explore."

"It was a good idea," she said. "But to tell you the truth, I would have rather just found a hotel with a pool, but whatever . . ."

We ate dinner, then walked back to the car to get our suitcases. Minutes later we were in the room, and Linda started getting Angela ready for bed while I went over my directions for the next day.

"The woman at the desk said that they have a closed-circuit station on the TV," I said. "They play a movie downstairs and it shows on Channel 3 in every room. Tonight they're showing a movie I saw when I was with the Franciscans: *Brother Sun, Sister Moon*. It's a movie about Saint Francis. It's one of my favorite films of all time."

"Let me get her in bed before you turn it on," Linda said. "She's really tired, so I don't think it's going to take very long."

Fifteen minutes later the movie started and we were settling in together on the bed. The Franco Zefferelli film reminded me of who I once was when I was younger and overflowing with the desire to serve the world, and I was anxious to share it with Linda. Almost as soon as the movie started, I felt it working on my consciousness, but not in the gentle way I imagined. The story of Saint Francis stirred a part of me that had been sleeping for years, the part that knew why I was born—to make a difference in the world and to live an extraordinary life. It showed me just how far my own life had drifted from that ideal. I loved my family and was happy I'd married Linda, but the thought of selling adjustable beds for the rest of my life filled me with absolute dread. I thought about the unhappy men in their forties and fifties who worked the same job. If I ended up like them, living check to check and selling something I didn't believe in, then I didn't know what I'd do. I thought of Martin Lloyd, who had committed suicide the previous year, only forty-five at the time but without hope. Would I end up like him if I stayed, lost and forgotten by life and the dreams I let die?

There was still a half hour left in the film, but I couldn't stay. I stood up and put on my jacket.

"Where are you going?" Linda asked me, clearly surprised.

"I just need to get some air," I said. "There's something I left in the car that I'll need in the morning. I'm going to find it before I get too tired."

I turned and walked out of the room, closing the door behind me. I felt my older self follow, floating behind as I walked down the hallway.

"Why did you leave like that?" I felt the older Linda ask me. I could tell that she was confused by everything she was seeing.

"Because I couldn't watch anymore. I remember that moment like it was yesterday. Watching that film reminded me who I was and why I was alive, and it also showed me how far I had gone away from that. It wasn't your fault, Linda . . . I was the one who let it happen."

"This feels like a turning point," she said. "This was where your life changed and starting moving in a different direction, wasn't it?"

"Yes, it was, but I'm not sure I like the result, at least part of it."

We watched as I walked outside and lit a cigarette. At this point we were hovering in front of my younger self, and I saw what looked like utter terror on my face. I walked at a brisk speed, but knew that I wasn't going anywhere intentionally. It almost looked like I was drunk, though I knew that I'd had nothing to drink that night. I weaved between trees and wondered if my younger self was about to fall down. Then suddenly I stopped and stood looking straight ahead. It was as if a feeling of deep peace suddenly overcame me. I stood there for a few seconds, then throwing the cigarette on the ground, turned around and walked back toward the car. After fumbling through my pocket for the keys, I opened the door and started the engine. The car backed out of the space with more speed than necessary, and I sped out of the lot toward the road. Seconds later the car disappeared down the drive, and I felt myself shift uneasily above the scene.

"Where are you going?" Linda asked me.

"I don't even know where I went," I said. "I'm not being evasive . . . I really don't remember. To tell you the truth, I don't think I had any idea where I was going even then. Part of me wanted to keep driving all the way back to Chicago. I may have even started in that direction."

"How long were you away?"

I felt my insides freeze up, not wanting to answer her. I had committed a terrible sin against the woman I loved, and now the same woman was asking me to explain. It was the one thing I felt most guilty about, the moment I made a mistake that cost more than I could have imagined at the time. There was no way for me to know at the time, but it was the beginning of the end of our marriage.

"I didn't come back till about noon the next day," I finally said. "I couldn't stand the idea that I was throwing my life away, but I also couldn't stand the thought of abandoning my family. The seed was planted that night, though, and nothing was ever the same."

"What did I say when you came back?"

"You were furious, of course. You thought something terrible had happened, like any sane person would have. I spent the next day trying to explain that other than my marriage, my life was meaningless. I had to quit my job and do something that would make a difference in the world. I didn't know what it was at the time, but I knew we had to get away. It was the last thing you wanted to hear. You were happy with the way things were. You didn't have to work, and had Angela to take care of. It was perfect, but I was drowning, and I didn't know what to do about it."

"What happened next?"

"Two weeks later we packed everything into a U-Haul and left Chicago. In the end we found a compromise—to go to Oregon and work for Ken Keyes at the personal-growth college he started. It wasn't what you really wanted, but it was better than living on an Indian reservation. That's what *I* wanted."

I felt the familiar sucking sensation and realized we were leaving the scene to return to the barn. Seconds later we were soaring through space, and I was grateful to be finally leaving the shrine. I also had the sensation that Linda was quieter than she had been before, as if she was thinking deeply about everything she saw through my eyes. It filled me with a strange fear, not unlike what I felt when I watched myself drive away in the car toward something I could not possibly understand at the time.

Was I losing her again? She saw what I did and now she understands why she never wanted me back, even though I tried to make up for my mistake for so many years. I was about to lose her for a second time, and there didn't seem to be anything I could do about it. As we soared through the clouds moving back toward the barn, I felt my heart begin to sink.

How many times do I have to pay? I asked myself.

CHAPTER NINETEEN

When I opened my eyes, we were back in the barn and Linda was looking at me with a sad expression.

"What are you thinking?" I asked her.

"I was thinking that it must have been a terrible thing for you to watch," she said, surprising me. I was sure that she would be angry about what I had done and how it had affected her and Angela. Instead, her thoughts were with *me*, as if this whole thing had been orchestrated for my benefit.

"It was terrible," I said, "but not as terrible as it was for you. The rug had just been pulled out from under your feet. You thought you were going on a little vacation, but instead your husband freaked out and started down the path of complete uncertainty."

"I'm sure it was hard, and I can imagine that there were incredible sacrifices you would've had to make if you had stayed," she said.

"Incredible sacrifices?" I asked her. "I'm not sure what you mean."

"Well, you're telling me that if you'd stayed in the marriage that you wouldn't have been able to accomplish many of the things you wanted to. You said that you felt a strong desire to make a difference in the world. Is that what you were saying?"

"I do remember feeling that," I said to her as I sat back in my chair. "I remember that I felt this draw to do something big and accomplish something extraordinary, and that I definitely wasn't moving in that direction at the time."

"No, you weren't. You were locked in a marriage and a family that were stopping you from having the impact on the world you wanted. You wanted to write books and make movies, but that wasn't going to happen if you stayed."

I felt a knot developing in my stomach, and a heavy feeling begin to weigh me down. She was expressing every justification I had treasured for over two decades, all the righteous excuses that made me seem almost noble for wanting to leave the marriage. *I wanted to save the world. I wanted to leave my mark.* It all made sense at the time, but as Linda recounted the reasons, they seemed to be losing altitude.

"Yes, it probably wouldn't have happened," I finally said.

"There's only one question I want to ask you," she said, her eyes filled with compassion. "If that's true . . . if you couldn't stay married to me and still do all those things . . . then why did you regret your decision for so long? Why did you try so hard to get me back and regret so many of the decisions you made while I was still alive?"

It was like I had just been shot through the heart. I knew the answer to her question, but I couldn't admit it out loud. I wanted to tell her that I was wrong, and that I made the whole thing up. My desire to leave the marriage had nothing to do with my wanting to make a mark on the world. It was all a cop-out, a justification that made me look good while leaving a family that loved me. The reality was that I was frightened out of my mind. I was twenty-five years old and felt completely insecure with who I was and what I was doing, and in the end I didn't feel fit to be married and raise a family. The world I had created was closing in around me, and I didn't know what to do about it. When we were together in St. Louis, I saw an opportunity and I took it. In the end it had nothing to do with me fulfilling my destiny. It was nothing more than a frenzied attempt to escape and run away.

The sound of the hypnotist's voice rang in my ears. "It's time to let go and fall into a deep sleep where everything is calm and relaxed." I looked up at the stage and saw that he had a new group of people with him and they, like the others, were quickly falling under his spell.

"There's one more question I want to ask you," Linda said, pulling my attention back to the table. "How does everything you just told me relate to my being killed?"

"How does it relate? It doesn't relate at all. That all happened eighteen years before you were killed, so how could they relate?"

"Don't think about it logically," she said. "Think about it from your heart, from your emotions. How were they similar?"

The words came out of my mouth so fast that I couldn't interpret or stop them, and the shock wave they sent through my body nearly knocked me off balance. I tried to stop them, but they were already following her instructions and completely caught me off guard.

"They killed your body, but I killed our marriage," I

said as tears began rolling down my cheeks. "I killed it by being so self-centered and stupid. My wanting to leave had nothing to do with the things I said . . . nothing to do with wanting to make an impact on the world. I was scared! I didn't know what else to do! If I didn't screw things up then they never would have had a chance to hurt you. You were murdered because of me . . . *because I wasn't there to save you*."

Linda's hand reached for mine as I collapsed on the table and began to weep. All the noise in the room merged in a cacophony of sound that shook the inside of my body, and I squeezed her hand hoping it would hold me together. For the first time I realized why I was there, and what I had come to learn. I thought I was there to forgive the men who killed Linda, but in reality I was there to forgive myself.

"It's okay," she said to me as she leaned forward. "You didn't do anything wrong . . . that's what you need to finally see. You were doing the best you could at the time. Now it's time for you to relax and heal that place within you that hasn't been able to let go."

"But I can't let go of it," I said. "I'm the one who's responsible. I've been so locked in this pain and guilt that I wasn't able to take responsibility for my role in it. It was too overpowering. I was the one . . . in the end, it was all because I wasn't strong enough."

She put her hand under my chin and gently lifted my head so she could see in my eyes.

"But you're strong enough now," she said. "If there's one lesson you can learn from everything that's happening here, it's that time isn't the impenetrable wall you thought it was. You can heal the past by choosing to heal yourself right now. I wasn't killed because of anything you did.

What happened to me had nothing to do with you. It was important for you to understand why you made the choice you made, and now that you understand, it's time for you to move past it. It's time for you to forgive yourself."

"I don't know if I can forgive myself."

She paused for a moment, then said: "I need you to see that this isn't just for this one moment. It has to do with many other things you can't understand right now."

"What do you mean?" I asked, looking up at her.

She paused again and looked straight into my eyes as if there was something she wanted to say but wasn't sure how. I was at the brink of discovering the reason all this was happening, and I didn't want to stop there. My eyes pleaded with her to continue.

"Do you remember the car?" she finally asked. "What happened there?"

"You said that there was a timeline where the car went over the edge and we all died, and another where we didn't."

"Yes . . . as long as you hold on to the pain, you can't set the other part of yourself free. Do you understand what I'm saying to you?"

"I'm still lost," I said. "What do you mean?"

"I told you that the only thing we take with us from one world to the next is love, right? Well, that's true, but there's also something that keeps us from feeling that love even though it's all around us—guilt. If you're not able to let go of the guilt you feel, then you can't move into the world where you belong. Do you see what I'm saying?"

"No, I really don't. Are you saying that the guilt I've been feeling about what happened to you has been limiting

THE BARN DANCE 🏚

the aspect of me that went over the cliff and died? But how is that possible?"

"It's possible because everything's connected," she said, grabbing hold of my arm as if she was desperate for me to understand. "It's not that there's one part of you here and another completely separate part that's in the world. There's only one, and the decisions you make in one place are experienced in the other. You can't possibly comprehend this intellectually, and that's why I keep telling to you to try to understand it with your heart. That's the only place it will make any sense."

"So where am I, then? You keep telling me that the reason I saw the car is because there's an aspect of me that's dead just like you . . . so where is that *me?*"

"Where do you think he is?" she asked. "You keep talking about it like you're somewhere else, as if it's not happening right now. It's time for you to see the truth . . . that the answer is right in front of you. *It's in front of you right now.*"

Her words cut through me, and I felt a sensation like the tumblers of a lock falling into place. In an instant everything made perfect sense. Everything I had experienced since I arrived at the cliff, as well as everything that happened at the barn, suddenly became clear. I fell back into my chair and took a deep breath.

"It's right here," I said. "It's all right in front of me. This is the aspect of me that died, isn't it? I only thought I was still alive because I didn't want to face the guilt I felt. That's why I'm here now. I'm not walking between two different worlds. I've been here the whole time."

"Yes," she said, "you've been here with me the whole time."

"What about the part of me that's not in Heaven?"

"There's no part of you that's not in Heaven, Jimmy, but it is possible to believe that you're in between."

"In between?" I repeated. "How can I be in between Heaven and Earth?"

Linda looked at me again as if there was something she wanted to say but couldn't. Her soft features seemed to disappear, and a look of sadness filled her eyes. I was trying to digest everything at once, but there was something more that she seemed to be avoiding.

"What are you not telling me?" I asked her.

She looked back at me with sad eyes. "I'm sorry. What I wanted to say is that you can believe that you're in between, though it's actually not possible. You've always been here, but you were afraid. You weren't able to let go, at least the aspect of you that was in the car when it went over. That meant you weren't able to move completely away from this world into the next—into Heaven."

"I wasn't able to follow you through the door at the end of the night with the rest of you . . . is that it? So I've been in Purgatory?"

Once again she looked away from me, as if the question was bigger than I realized. "In a way, yes . . . a self-imposed Purgatory."

"And what about Richard? What's his role in all this?"

I looked over at him and realized he had been staring at us the entire time. There was a glow around his body, as if he was somehow set apart from everything else that was happening. He smiled at me, and in that moment I understood who he was.

"Well, Richard is . . . I guess you could say that he's your angel," Linda said. "He's the one who's been watching over you." She reached over and put her hand over mine. "You were never alone, don't you see. You just had to get to the point where you felt safe forgiving yourself. It was never about the men who killed me. It was always about you."

My head was swimming, and I didn't know what to think. If Linda was right and I really was experiencing the aspect of me that went over the cliff, did that mean that everything else was an illusion? Had I only imagined the last three years?

"No, you didn't imagine any of it," Linda said to me as if she could read everything I was thinking. "Everything you remember did happen and it's all still waiting there for you, if that's what you want."

"So the aspect of me that didn't go over the cliff. That person's real, right?"

"Yes, he is."

"And Angela and Heather made it as well, right?"

"Yes, they made it as well."

"So where is that happening? All this time I thought that I was the one living in a human body, but I'm no different from anyone else here at the barn."

"Except that you have the ability to choose where you want to be and what you want to experience. If you want to, you can move on, or you can go back and experience the other world. It's a remarkable gift, Jimmy, one that very few of us ever get."

I was not prepared for this, or for the sudden realization that I actually had a choice. If I chose to stay conscious of this reality I was experiencing in the barn, then I would be able to stay with Linda and love her in the way I was never able to when she was alive. But at the same time, Angela was waiting for me on the other side and I wanted to experience that as well. For the first time in my life, I was faced with a choice that was both simple and impossible.

"Why can't I do both?" I asked her. "Isn't it possible for me to be aware of both realities at the same time, staying here with you but also being back in Oregon with Angela?"

"You can only be consciously aware of one, but you're experiencing both at the same time. That's the clearest I can make it. I know it doesn't make sense."

"So I have to choose which one I'll see," I said to myself, finally grasping everything she said. "And how do I do that?"

"You just have to let go," she said, "and let it happen. It's really very simple." Then she paused, took a deep breath, and said: "And it looks like I have to do the same thing."

"What do you mean?" I asked her. The faraway look had returned to her eyes as if she was watching a world no one else could see. It was as if she was holding something back, as if she didn't want anyone else to see what was happening to her. "Linda, I have to ask you something. Is there anything you're not telling me?"

She sat back in her chair and looked at me. "First of all, you need to know that I haven't been holding anything back. If I seem a little distracted, it's only because I'm realizing something for the first time, just as you are. It seems that this journey was for both of us, not just you. It just surprised me, that's all."

"Tell me more," I said. "What do you mean by that?"

"Let's just say that you weren't the only one who had something to learn," she said as she looked away. "All this time I thought that we were here for your lesson, for what you needed, but I guess that was a little naïve. In the end we're all here to learn . . . it's something that never ends. You see, a moment ago when we were talking, I remembered something from my life, something that was holding me back, and something that I have to let go of now."

"You had a lesson to learn as well," I repeated. "Can you tell me what you remembered?"

"First of all, I have to ask you a question," she said. "If there was one thing that stopped us from getting back together, what would you say it was?"

The answer was easy. "You weren't able to forgive me for abandoning you. It was something that you were so sensitive about, and when I left you, first in St. Louis then in Oregon, you weren't able to let it go. I think it was always in the back of your mind and you thought I would do it again. No matter what I did to show you that I was changed, you couldn't see me."

"I couldn't see you . . . yes, that's it. And so I held on to it because I felt betrayed. Then when I was in Evanston and I was stabbed, I felt alone again, completely alone . . . as if I had been abandoned for the last time. But you see, that's not what happened, and I only now just realized it."

"Please tell me," I said to her. "You can't stop there. What did you realize?"

"I'm not sure I can tell you," she said. "It's not that I don't want you to know . . . I do. I just think it might be easier if I showed you."

"You want to show me, like I was showing you events from our lives before? It works both ways?"

"Yes, it does, but I'm warning you that this may be

painful for you to watch. If we do decide to go through with this, then it might be more than you can take."

"I can take anything at this point," I said. "I feel like we've come so far already. We can't stop now!"

"Let me help you if I can."

She reached over and took my hand. "Then we'll go. All I can say is that you have to remain calm no matter what happens. Do you understand what I'm saying?"

I felt my insides begin to shake. "Yes, I really do understand."

"Then look into my eyes and take a deep breath," she said. "What we're about to witness is the final piece of the puzzle, and it's not going to be easy."

CHAPTER TWENTY

We were soaring over the north side of Chicago, and I instantly realized that something had changed. I was inside Linda instead of the other way around. We were flying over buildings just along Lake Michigan, and when we came to Calvary Cemetery, I knew that we were entering into Evanston. I felt a dark fear begin to rise inside me when I realized this. Why are we going back to Evanston? I had been avoiding that city ever since Linda had been killed. There's no reason for us to be there, unless of course . . .

"Linda, I can't do this," I said to her as we continued moving north.

"You can do anything," I felt her say. "You just need to trust me . . . when we see this, everything will make sense for both of us."

We began shifting to the west until we were in the neighborhood where Linda and Angela lived for many years. Seconds later I realized we were floating over their former apartment, and we began slowly descending until the roof evaporated beneath our feet and we found ourselves in the living room. We hesitated there for a moment wondering what we were meant to see. I looked around and saw blood on the floor and on the walls, but Linda was nowhere to be found.

"I think I know where I am," I felt Linda say to me.

We began moving toward the two bedrooms and the bathroom at the end of he hall. As we passed Linda's bedroom, I looked inside. No one was there. Then we slowly approached Angela's bedroom, stopping when we arrived at the front of the door.

"Oh my God!" I gasped when I looked inside.

I saw her lying across Angela's bed in a pool of blood, her eyes open wide. I could feel the older Linda react as well, as if seeing herself dying or even dead in the room was an incomprehensible shock. Then as I looked, I suddenly realized that she was not dead at all, but still alive. A slight movement in her chest told me that she was breathing, and then I saw her arm move up toward her neck, a futile attempt to stop the bleeding. It was a terrifying scene, and if I had been in control of the body we shared, I would have turned away so I didn't have to see it. But this was Linda's journey, and I had no choice but to watch it unfold.

Then we heard a crash in the other room and the sound of men rushing into the apartment.

"Is there anyone here?" I heard a man's voice say. "Is there anyone in the apartment?" Then a large man rushed past us with his gun pulled. He wore a blue button-up shirt with his badge attached to his belt, and I realized he was a detective. He saw Linda slumped over the bed and ran to her, laying her gently onto the floor.

"I found her," he screamed to the other men. "She's in the bedroom."

Two other officers in uniform ran into the room, but by then the detective was holding Linda in his arms trying to stop the bleeding. Both hands were over her neck, and the blood seemed to slow.

"One of you go outside and show the paramedics where we are as soon as they get here," the detective said. The officer ran out of the room, and the other stood with one hand over his mouth.

"I'm still alive," I felt Linda say to me. "I didn't die right away. He's trying to save me."

I tried to speak, but the words wouldn't come. I was paralyzed watching the one thing in the world I never wanted to know anything about. Whenever someone tried to tell me details, I made them stop, usually because Angela was also present, but mostly because I didn't want to hear them myself. And now I was standing there watching my wife die. I knew how this ended. There was no hope.

"Just hold on," the detective said to her. "Help is on the way. Just hold on."

He looked at her with such tenderness, as if he was holding his own sister or wife in his arms. It was only then that Linda looked up at him. She couldn't talk, but her eyes said more than words ever could. Someone was with her. She wasn't alone. No matter what happened, she wouldn't die alone in her daughter's room. "Just hang in there," he said to her again, and I saw what looked like a slight smile cross her lips.

And then, as if watching a movie, the smile dissolved and her eyes lost their focus. Her head fell back onto his arm, and Linda died. Everything was silent. No one moved in the room, including us. Then I felt us begin to float up toward the ceiling and out of the room. We soared over the city and disappeared into the clouds. Seconds later I opened my eyes to see we were back in the barn.

CHAPTER TWENTY-ONE

Tears were running down Linda's face and I heard her take a long, staggered breath. I reached over and wrapped my arms around her and held her tight, and it felt more wonderful than I could have imagined. Seconds earlier I was watching her die on the floor of her apartment, and now I was holding the very same woman who felt healthy and alive. I had given up trying to make sense of everything that happened in the barn. At that point all I could do was be grateful I was there, grateful to be holding her again, and grateful that at least in one reality, she was still alive.

"It's all right," I said to her. "That was too much for you to see."

She pulled back and looked at me. "I'm not crying because I saw myself die. I'm crying because I know why I'm here . . . what lesson I had to learn."

"What lesson could you possibly have to learn here?" I asked her. "There was no sense to it . . . no logic or reason."

"It's not meant to be logical," she said. "The lessons of our souls aren't the same as the mind's logic. You told me before that I felt abandoned when you left me, and that's why I was never able to forgive you and see that you had changed?"

"Yes, I remember."

"I've been holding on to that feeling even here," she said as if it finally made sense. "I considered my death to be the ultimate abandonment, especially because I died alone with you and Angela in Minneapolis. Once again you weren't there for me . . . or at least that's what I thought."

"I'm sorry, Linda, but I . . ."

"No, it has nothing to do with you," she said. "It has to do with me realizing that things don't always go the way we want, and the people we love aren't always there when we need them. And when I realized that, then I was able to remember. I remembered that I didn't die alone like I thought I did. That was Detective Glue. I was looking into his eyes when I died. Someone was with me, and I wasn't abandoned at all. Now I can let that go because I know the truth. That's why I was led here, why I had to come to the barn. I had a lesson to learn just like you did."

"But I don't understand," I said, desperately trying to understand what was happening. "You're in Heaven. I thought that when you're here you're free and you don't have to go through these things anymore."

"If there's only one thing I hope you'll learn from being here," she said, "it's that Heaven isn't a place you go after you die. Heaven is all around you . . . here in the barn, back in Oregon, and wherever else you find yourself. And because Heaven is everywhere, you only have to open your eyes to see it. That's the key to life. To do that you need to learn what's holding you back. Do you understand what I'm saying?"

"No, I don't," I said. "I've been coming here to be with you and all these other people who lived either long or short lives on Earth, and now they come here to the barn to remember who they were. I thought they did that because . . . to tell you the truth, I'm not really sure why."

"They come here to learn," she said, "whether they realize it or not. I came to learn that I was never really alone, and that it's time to let go of the wounds and scars that held me back from realizing the truth. Everyone in this room is the same, they all have their lessons, and yes, they are in Heaven . . . just like you."

I tried to wrap my mind around everything she said, but it was so far outside any frame of reference I had that it only left me more confused.

"I'm just like all of you," I said. "I'm here because I wasn't able to forgive myself, and that kept me from moving on. I died just like you and everyone else in the barn."

"But there is a difference," she said. "You're also here because you can make a choice. You can stay here and move on with me, or you can go back to Angela and remember the aspect of yourself that didn't go over the cliff. You're in a very unique position because you have the ability to choose."

"I don't feel like I can make a choice," I said. "It's impossible. If I stay here, then I get to move on with you, and if I go back, I'll get to be with Angela. I still don't understand why I can't be conscious of both."

"I don't know what to tell you, Jimmy. I know what I've decided. Now that I've seen what really happened, I want to let go of that part of me that's so afraid of being abandoned. That's what kept me from being totally fulfilled . . . in both life and death. I'm choosing to move on. And you have to choose as well. All I can tell you is that either way, you're choosing love. Maybe that makes it a little easier for you."

I felt a hand on my shoulder and heard a man's voice say: "I think this gentleman is a perfect subject for our experiment. Why don't we encourage him to join me onstage."

I suddenly realized that the hypnotist was standing behind our table and was looking straight at me. His hand was held out, and I realized that he was inviting me onto the stage.

"No, I can't," I said. "I need to stay here with her."

"It's okay, Jimmy. I'll be right here. Go ahead."

"It looks like we have our next volunteer," Lance said as I stood up and took his hand. I followed him to the stage as everyone clapped, but I never lost sight of Linda. Whatever was about to happen, I didn't want to lose her.

"Are you ready, sir?" he asked me.

"I'm not sure if I am or not, but I'm going to say yes."

"Very good. I'll ask you to take a seat in this chair and just relax. I can assure you that nothing's going happen beyond your control, and you're not going to go anywhere that isn't *safe* or *calm.*"

He said the words *safe* and *calm* with a very different inflection than the other words, and even though I was aware of this trick, I found myself instantly relaxing in my chair. My eyes were wide open, and I was looking at Linda, who was smiling broadly at me.

"You're going to go to a *deep* world now that is so welcoming and so vast that you can't resist its urge. It's the world of your *deeper* mind, where all your memories and all your dreams reside. Soon you'll feel your eyes getting *heavier* and you'll allow them to close, but only when you feel it happen on its own."

I tried to stare at Linda, but the impulse to close my eyes was growing so strong that I couldn't resist. I slowly let them droop shut, and did my best to stay conscious of my surroundings.

"Now I'm going to ask you a couple of questions, and you're free to answer me. Can you hear my voice?"

My words felt like they came from far in the distance. "Yes, I can."

"And do you feel comfortable and relaxed?"

"Yes, I do."

"That's excellent. Now I'm going to ask you to take one deep breath, and to let it out very slowly. As you let the breath out, you're going to say in your mind: 'I AM safe . . . I AM home.' Do you understand these instructions?"

"Yes, I do."

"Okay, so take a deep breath and slowly let it out, repeating the words I just gave you in your mind."

As I exhaled the breath I thought the words "I AM safe . . . I AM home." As I did, it felt as though I was fading away, as if I were losing myself and didn't know where I was. I wanted to open my eyes and use Linda as a rock that would hold me in place. I didn't want to leave her, and yet another part of me wanted to be back with Angela, to help her become the amazing adult Linda and I always imagined she would become. I felt myself being pulled between these two desires, and I didn't know which side would win. Then at the last second, I realized that I could open my eyes slightly, and I looked in the direction of the table where Linda and I had been sitting moments earlier.

I saw Linda, but she wasn't alone. She was talking to another man, someone who seemed familiar but I couldn't be sure. Then I realized who it was she was talking to. It was me! Linda was at the table holding my hand, and we were deep in conversation. I could feel the love emanating from the two of us, and it soothed my heart in a way I had never experienced before.

Then as I watched them, they stood up and walked away from the table, then toward the bright door on the other side of the barn. They walked toward it with their hands joined, then Linda reached out and opened it just wide enough to walk through. A second passed, and they were gone, disappearing from the barn forever.

I let my eyes close again and drifted off to sleep.

CHAPTER TWENTY-TWO

I opened my eyes again and discovered that the barn was gone and I was sitting against the tree where I'd first met Richard. There was no hypnotist, no barn, and worst of all, no Linda. For several minutes I sat there trying to understand what had happened and why I was there at all. Had I been transported back to the spot where the strange adventure began, or had I been asleep the entire time dreaming of a world that didn't really exist? I was certain that it *did* exist, and that I really had spent the last three days in a barn somewhere between Heaven and Earth. I also knew that I had made a decision, one that would influence me for the rest of my life. I could have stayed there if I'd wanted, but instead I chose to go home and continue raising our daughter.

But that wasn't where the story ended. There was another aspect of me that was in Heaven with Linda, loving her just as I wished I could have while she was alive. That thought was enough for me. In that moment, it was the only thing that felt real.

I stood up and looked around, half expecting to find Richard walking out of the forest with a cup of coffee in his hands. But I was alone with only the sound of the nearby stream. There was no one there to tell me if I was meant to leave or await further instructions. In my heart I knew that it was over, whatever it had been. After about a half hour, the sun began to rise over the hills and I started to move back in the direction I suspected I would find the cliff. I traveled only ten minutes before I found it, and I began climbing to the top.

Once at the road, I walked back to the original spot where we had nearly gone over three and a half years earlier. Now, after everything I had been through, I knew that I was right . . . we really did lose control of the car that night, and the BMW at the bottom of the cliff was the proof. I stepped out to the edge and looked over, wanting to see it one last time.

It was gone.

The car I saw before had vanished, as if it didn't exist at all. I finally came to the point where I began questioning my own sanity. What had I really seen, and what was just an illusion? If there was an answer, it wasn't coming to me at that moment. I had no choice but to walk back to my car and begin the long drive home.

I arrived back in Portland two days later and began trying to piece everything together. Though it was impossible for me to determine what it all meant, there was one thing I knew for sure—something had changed inside me. I called Angela and told her I was home, then wondered if I would ever tell her about the experience in the barn. I wanted her to know that her mother was still there and that she was waiting for us. I also wanted her to know that we were both there with her, even though that didn't make any sense at all. The mystery had never been fully resolved, but I knew I was in the right place. It was time to forgive.

"What would you say if I told you that I saw your mother?" I asked Angela.

I had arrived back in Portland, and we were driving to a restaurant in the Pearl District. When I'd left a week earlier to begin the strange odyssey, I hadn't told my daughter the real purpose of my trip. She thought I was going to Ashland to visit friends, which of course was true, but I left out the real and most important detail—I intended to return to the cliff. There was no need to worry her, and even if I wanted to I didn't know what to say. At the time, I thought I was losing my mind and that the cliff held some kind of undetermined power over me. Now I knew that it wasn't the cliff at all, but a small barn in the center of an unpredictable forest where Heaven and Earth somehow blend together and where the most magical dance in the world takes place each and every night. I still couldn't explain what really happened, but I knew it was real. What I experienced wasn't a dream at all, but a miracle that changed my life forever.

"What do you mean you saw Mom?" she asked. "Do you mean you saw her in a dream?"

I paused for a few seconds before answering. Did she really need to know all the details, and even if I told her, would she even believe me? The most important detail was that Linda was still with us, and that we were also with her. And yet I also knew that the details of my adventure were important, so I took a deep breath and began my story. "Are you serious?" she asked when I finished. "Did that really happen?"

"I can tell you that I did go back to the cliff," I said, "and that I did see a car at the bottom where we almost went over. I can also say that what I experienced at the barn felt completely real, not like a dream at all, even though I woke up the next morning leaning against a tree. Most important, though, I know I was with Linda . . . there's no question in my mind about that. The things she said changed my life because now I know that death isn't real and that we really do get to be with the ones we love forever. Love never ends, but keeps growing and expanding forever."

I looked over at Angela and realized she was trying to hide her face from me. Then she turned toward me, and I saw tears running down her cheeks.

"Did she say anything about me?" she asked. "Does she even remember me?"

I reached over and took her hand. "She told me to tell you that she's proud of you, and that she'll see you again. It was her promise. In fact, you're already there with her, and so am I. It doesn't make any sense . . . I know that . . . but it's the one thing I'm certain of. This universe is so much larger than we think it is, and there are mysteries the intellect will never be able to comprehend. But the heart already knows they're true. That's what I learned at the barn, and I know it's already changing my life. I also know that I chose to be here with you, and to live an extraordinary life. I'm going to do it for her, and for everyone else I love."

She wiped her tears away with her sleeve. "I don't really understand what happened to you," she said, "and it's pretty hard to believe. But it does make me feel better, and that's the only thing I care about. If Mom really is out there watching me and waiting for me to be with her, then it means she really isn't gone. That makes me feel pretty good."

A month later I decided to go for a drive. After a bit of research I was able to locate the one man that could help me make sense of everything that happened. I drove through the suburbs of Portland until I arrived at the house of Marcus Oakes in Beaverton. He didn't know I was coming, and he didn't know who I was, but we did have a mutual friend.

"Can I help you?" he asked when he answered the door. He was a kind-looking man with short gray hair and sad eyes. At first I thought I'd made a mistake but decided to follow through just to make sure.

"Sir, my name is James Twyman, and I think I have some information you might want. May I come in for a moment?"

He stepped aside and let me in the front door, obviously suspicious of my sudden appearance. Then he motioned for me to sit down in a chair in the living room, and he sat across from me. I looked around for any sign that would show me I wasn't crazy. The house was neat and modestly furnished, and felt as if it hadn't changed or been redecorated in many years. That's when I saw what I was looking for, a picture of an elderly woman on one of the bookshelves. She was the reason I came. Martha!

"Mr. Oakes, what I'm about to tell you is going to sound very strange and hard to believe, but I promise you that it's very true. I've never met you before, and you haven't met me, and I also don't know anything about you, except one thing. I know that you lost your wife, Martha."

"What do you know about Martha?" he asked, suddenly defensive.

"I don't know much at all, only that I have a message for you from her. I know how crazy that sounds, but I have to tell you this. She wants you to know that she loves you very much and that she's waiting for you on the other side. I guess you could say that I met her there myself and that . . ."

"Get the hell out of my house!" he yelled, standing up and facing me. "Who do you think you are, and what do you want? You think you can just come into my house and give me this story and get some money . . . is that it? Well you can forget it. Just get the hell out!"

"Mr. Oakes, there's one last thing. Martha told me you wouldn't believe me, so she gave me something to say. She told me to have you look in the butterfly drawer."

He suddenly stopped and turned white.

"What did you just say to me?" he asked.

"Your wife told me that you wouldn't believe me, so she told me something that I don't understand at all. She said to tell you to look inside the butterfly drawer, then you would listen."

He sat back down in the chair and let out a long sigh. Then he looked at me and motioned for me to sit back down as well.

"I didn't think it was possible," he said after a long pause. "I wanted to believe that there was more after all this, but it's so hard to wrap your brain around. But the butterfly drawer?"

"What does it mean, sir?"

He looked up at me with eyes filled with both sorrow and hope. "No one in this world knows about the butterfly drawer except Martha and me. It was a gift I gave her on our first anniversary. She loved that little thing . . . just a little box with a drawer where she kept her jewelry. Well, after she died, I didn't feel it was right to keep wearing my wedding ring, so I took it off and put it there. The butterfly drawer is where I keep the most prized possession in my life, son."

"Then you know . . . you know that she's still here with you. That's all I wanted to say. She wanted you to know."

As I said these words, I felt a strange sensation that was almost impossible to describe. If Martha was watching Marcus Oakes, then it meant Linda was watching me. And one day I would be back with her, and Angela would be there as well, even though there was another part of us that was already at her side.

I left the house a few minutes later. As I walked to the car, I thought about Linda and everything she'd said to me when we were together. She had been right all along. *Love really is the only thing we bring with us.*

THE END

ABOUT THE AUTHOR

James F. Twyman is the best-selling author of numerous books, including *The Moses Code, The Kabbalah Code,* and *The Proof.* He's also an internationally renowned "Peace Troubadour" who has a reputation for drawing millions of people together in prayer to positively influence crises throughout the world. He has been invited by leaders of countries such as Iraq, Northern Ireland, South Africa, Bosnia, Croatia, and Serbia to perform The Peace Concert—often while conflicts raged in those areas; and he has performed at the United Nations, the Pentagon, and more.

James is the executive producer and co-writer of the feature film *Indigo,* and the director of *Indigo Evolution* and the documentary *The Moses Code.* He is also the founder of The Seminary of Spiritual Peacemaking, which has ordained over 500 ministers from around the world.

Websites: **www.TheMosesCode.com**
and **www.JamesTwyman.com**

We hope you enjoyed this Hay House book. If you'd like to receive our online catalog featuring additional information on Hay House books and products, or if you'd like to find out more about the Hay Foundation, please contact:

Hay House, Inc., P.O. Box 5100, Carlsbad, CA 92018-5100

(760) 431-7695 or **(800) 654-5126**
(760) 431-6948 (fax) or **(800) 650-5115 (fax)**
www.hayhouse.com® • **www.hayfoundation.org**

***

Published and distributed in Australia by: Hay House Australia Pty. Ltd., 18/36 Ralph St., Alexandria NSW 2015 • Phone: 612-9669-4299 • Fax: 612-9669-4144 www.hayhouse.com.au

Published and distributed in the United Kingdom by: Hay House UK, Ltd., 292B Kensal Rd., London W10 5BE • Phone: 44-20-8962-1230 • Fax: 44-20-8962-1239 www.hayhouse.co.uk

Published and distributed in the Republic of South Africa by: Hay House SA (Pty), Ltd., P.O. Box 990, Witkoppen 2068 • Phone/Fax: 27-11-467-8904 info@hayhouse.co.za • www.hayhouse.co.za

Published in India by: Hay House Publishers India, Muskaan Complex, Plot No. 3, B-2, Vasant Kunj, New Delhi 110 070 • Phone: 91-11-4176-1620 Fax: 91-11-4176-1630 • www.hayhouse.co.in

Distributed in Canada by: Raincoast, 9050 Shaughnessy St., Vancouver, B.C. V6P 6E5 • Phone: (604) 323-7100 • Fax: (604) 323-2600 • www.raincoast.com

***

Take Your Soul on a Vacation

Visit **www.HealYourLife.com®** to regroup, recharge,
and reconnect with your own magnificence.
Featuring blogs, mind-body-spirit news, and life-changing
wisdom from Louise Hay and friends.

Visit **www.HealYourLife.com** today!

DREAM DANCING

Now you can learn to communicate with
your loved ones who have passed to another world.

When James Twyman had the experience that led to him writing *The Barn Dance,* it didn't initially occur to him that there might be a process that could help others learn to communicate with their family or friends who have passed away. After considerable research and practice, he was able to produce a series of exercises that can help anyone accomplish similar results, leading to deep levels of healing and intimate discourse.

If you read this book and wondered if it was possible for you to enjoy a conversation with someone who has left this world, then you may consider participating in this magical course.

James has put together a home study program complete with recorded lessons and other valuable information that may allow you to reestablish dialogue with anyone you long to communicate with. If you believe that we are not truly separated by death, and that it is possible to enjoy profound relationships with loved ones even after they have passed, then we invite you to go to **www.jamestwyman.com** to receive more details. James will also be offering day-long and weekend retreats on this process, details of which will be available on the site.

There are shamanic practices that can teach us how to Dream-Dance our way into higher levels of communication with the very people we thought we would never experience again. These are ancient practices, and you can learn them within a very short period of time.

For complete information visit: **www.jamestwyman.com**

Mind Your Body,
Mend Your Spirit

Hay House is the ultimate resource for inspirational and health-conscious books, audio programs, movies, events, e-newsletters, member communities, and much more.

Visit **www.hayhouse.com**® today and nourish your soul.

UPLIFTING EVENTS
Join your favorite authors at live events in a city near you or log on to **www.hayhouse.com** to visit with Hay House authors online during live, interactive Web events.

INSPIRATIONAL RADIO
Daily inspiration while you're at work or at home. Enjoy radio programs featuring your favorite authors, streaming live on the Internet 24/7 at **HayHouseRadio.com**®. Tune in and tune up your spirit!

VIP STATUS
Join the Hay House VIP membership program today and enjoy exclusive discounts on books, CDs, calendars, card decks, and more. You'll also receive 10% off all event reservations (excluding cruises). Visit **www.hayhouse.com/wisdom** to join the Hay House Wisdom Community™.

Visit **www.hayhouse.com** and enter priority code 2723 during checkout for special savings!
(One coupon per customer.)